HIDDEN TREASURE

I. "Spring Flowers" Egg by Fabergé is made of red enamel on gold and set with rose diamonds. The flower basket is of diamond-studded platinum; flowers are carved in milky chalcedony with olivine centers set in green gold. The base is carved of bowenite. Made between 1885 and 1891, this Imperial Easter Egg was presented to Marie Feodorovna by her husband, Tsar Alexander III. It is signed: M.II. *(Ch. I)*

HIDDEN TREASURE

How and where to find it

by Jeanne Horn

BONANZA BOOKS · NEW YORK

146126

Library of Congress Catalog Card Number: 62-21610

This edition published by Bonanza Books,
a division of Crown Publishers, Inc.,
by arrangement with Arco Publishing Co., Inc.

Printed in the United States of America

(C)

FOREWORD

IN London, a bus driver finds a battered Renoir painting lying in a street; near New York, a map that Custer carried when he was killed, was located wrapped in a paper parcel; in Kansas City, an art restorer, cleaning the back of a Cézanne painting discovers another Cézanne painting on the reverse of the canvas; in San Francisco, a rare penny is found in a handful of change; in Wyoming, a musket ordered by George Washington is identified; and, in a St. Paul attic, the field notes of explorers Lewis and Clark are found. . . . These are but a few recent discoveries of artistic or historical materials. For each, there are hundreds of others.

The bus driver had never heard of Renoir, but he called a museum; the art restorer never suspected the existence of the second painting, but worked with extreme care; and the coin collector had made it a habit of examining every coin he received.

In all of these finds runs a common denominator that you will find in this book: each was authenticated by persons expert in specialized fields. Unless you are a collector, dealer, artist, or museum curator, you will experience difficulty in determining whether an article is rare and valuable, or commonplace. This demands knowledge that can only be acquired by much study and hard work, and an opinion can be as exacting as a medical diagnosis or legal brief. But you can and should be able to decide when to call an expert. This book is full of clues that will interest and help you, for whether you have an old airplane, a letter, a piano, or a cave, chances are, someone, somewhere will prize and want it.

Milton F. Perry
Museum Curator
Harry S. Truman Library

v

CONTENTS

ILLUSTRATIONS

COLOR PLATES

INTRODUCTION

E VERY day someone throws away a fortune because he does not know a lost treasure when he finds one.

Did you know that there is a missing stamp which is worth $100,000? That Benjamin Franklin invented a fan chair which has never been found? That there are antique cars worth thousands of dollars if we knew where they were?

Did you realize that there are missing Civil War stamps worth small fortunes even though Confederate money is worthless? That there are places in the United States where you can hunt for diamonds as men used to hunt once for gold? That there is war loot from World War II which still has not been located? That King Alfred's (English) Handbook is missing?

Or had you forgotten that not all of Cellini's works of art have been located? That Lincoln's letter to Mrs. Bixby would be worth $100,000 if it could be found? That the Great Table diamond, weighing two hundred and forty carats, has been missing since the seventeenth century? That there was a "skin" painting of Our Lady of Guadalupe stolen from a museum in Santa Fe, New Mexico, and never returned?

There are missing buttons, guns, autographs, gems, coins, paintings, violins, books, coffins, letters, snuffboxes, furniture, glassware, apostle spoons, ships' figureheads, hornbooks—and so on . . . and on . . . and on.

Anything can be a lost treasure! Even milady's fan, if it was decorated by such men as Watteau and Fragonard, can be worth a small fortune. Books, letters and Easter eggs—all of them valuable if you can find the right ones.

The trick, of course, is to be able to recognize a lost treasure when you find one. A bathtub can be a treasure—if it is Benjamin Franklin's slipper bath. Even the experts have been unable to find this one. Or a piece of paper can be worth a fortune—if it is a stock certificate or bond that has acquired a value you knew nothing about, issued long ago by companies since reorganized or boasting of belatedly gushing oil wells.

A rare signed mezzotint of yesteryear can actually be a collector's item. An old piece of furniture might turn out to be a part of the original furnishings of Mount Vernon. A drum might turn out to be a Revolutionary War Drum.

Or that funny-looking old manuscript in the attic might turn out to be one of the missing copies of the Magna Carta. When King John gave in to the barons in 1215 and acquiesced to their demands, the now famous Magna Carta was drawn up, and forty seven copies were made, one for every sheriff and one for every cathedral chapter. Yet until today only four copies have been found, or will ever be found—unless you can locate them and can recognize them when you do.

Everything has some value. Bottles and buttons, guns and furniture, books and pamphlets. They all have value, if they are the right ones and if you know a treasure when you see one. If, for example, you should find a copy of the Pennsylvania Gazette, do not throw it away. It might be a copy of the journal founded by Benjamin Franklin. As a matter of fact, never throw anything away. That old junk piece of furniture might be Chippendale. That dirty old painting might be a Renoir. That old gun might be a collectors' item.

Never give up. You never know when treasure might be right beside you. Not too long ago, in Texas, three men searched and worked for three days to find topaz. Finally, tired and discouraged, they gave up, but a woman accompanying them on their topaz hunt decided to take a walk before they all went home—and found a blue topaz weighing over two hundred carats.

Never belittle anything you find. The farmer who dug up a ring in his field and hung it on his dog's collar certainly belittled his find —until he discovered the ring was gold. As it turned out, the ring was not only gold but had belonged to Ethelswith, the sister of Alfred the Great.

It makes no difference how long this ring had been lost, nor how long any treasure is lost. If you will be able to recognize it when you see it, you have a good chance of finding it.

A group of German excavators working at Olympia, Greece, found Praxiteles' statue of Hermes that had been missing for over a thousand years. The famous Bayeux tapestry was found in the cathedral of Bayeux after having been lost for centuries. In Massachusetts a skeleton dressed in full armor, dating from a period before Columbus, was unearthed close by an ancient tower.

Nor does it matter what you happen to be engaged in when you find a fortune. You could be doing anything when you find treasure. A father and his son were playing a game of horseshoes in a vacant lot in Peterstown, West Virginia, when they found the thirty-four-carat Punch Jones diamond. A farmer was chasing his cow when he stumbled over a rock that turned out to be gold, the first of a million dollars' worth of this fabulous metal which was eventually taken from this spot.

There also is no limit to the places where treasure can be found. An auctioneer found an $89,000 prayer book in an old basket. The Bradford fragment, a portion of a New England Primer, was found in the binding of a newer book. A ten-thousand-pound, sixteenth century, marble table was found in the yard of an English housewrecker.

Treasure can be found almost anywhere. Even in the Leningrad Archives, where, according to one news report, were found manuscripts and letters of such men as Sir Walter Scott and James Fenimore Cooper. Or even in a junk pile in Scotland, where the missing Revere copperplate was found.

In a convent library, a lost fifteenth-century woodcut of Saint Christopher was rediscovered. In an attic, a woman found some old Lincoln letters worth thousands of dollars. An Arkansas farmer ploughed up a diamond weighing over two carats. A jade boulder weighing over a thousand pounds was found in California. The ring that Anne Hathaway allegedly gave to William Shakespeare was discovered in a field at Stratford-on-Avon.

WHAT is treasure? Treasure can be anything. A piece of paper, a diamond from a creekbed, a painting, a sheet of music or an old newspaper. If, during the heydey of the great showman, P. T. Barnum, a little boy could have found a male calico cat, Barnum would have paid him one thousand dollars for it. It is possible that while the professional treasure hunters were out digging for Captain Kidd's treasure chests or hot-footing it for the Lost Dutchman mine, neither of which they ever found, they passed up a thousand-dollar calico cat. For who would be so silly as to think a cat could be treasure? Well, I would—if another Barnum would make me an offer—and if I could find a male calico cat.

All this of course provided I knew that a calico cat was treasure. If you know treasure when you see it, you are on your way to fortune. But whatever you do, remember not to be like the treasure hunter in the anecdote told by Bennett Cerf in *Anything for a Laugh*.

This particular treasure hunter had located a letter signed by Thomas Jefferson, with a notation added by a man by the name of Button Gwinnett. Thinking that he would receive more for the letter if the notation were removed, he used ink eradicator on the spot where Button Gwinnett, one of the signers of the Declaration of Independence, had autographed it.

What he removed was a signature worth over fifty thousand dollars—and all because he did not know a lost treasure when he found one.

J. H.

Vallejo, Calif.
September, 1962

ACKNOWLEDGEMENT

I wish to thank all the numerous people who made this work possible. There were so many who gave so much of their time and their effort! Space, however, does not permit mention of all their names, so I am taking this shorter method to try to express my appreciation.

I would especially like to thank: John Walker, director, National Gallery of Art, Smithsonian Institution; A. Kenneth Snowman, Wartski's Jewelers, London; Milton F. Perry, Curator of the Museum, Harry S. Truman Library; C. A. Palmer, Insurance Company of North America Companies; R. Gerald McMurtry, director, the Lincoln National Life Foundation; Gordon Harmer, president, Harmer, Rooke and Co., Inc.; and Frederick R. Goff, Rare Book Division, Library of Congress.

HIDDEN TREASURE

I

THE EASTER EGG TREASURE

The Lost Art Works of Fabergé

E VEN an Easter egg can be worth a fortune—if it was designed by Fabergé, Court Jeweler to the Czar of Russia.

Easter eggs by Fabergé were not just another gift for Easter but very special creations made for the royal family of Russia—and made with such imagination and craftsmanship that the world has never before or since seen their like.

Fabergé was one of the greatest jewelers of his era. His shop in St. Petersburg, Russia, reached a height of fame unknown to other jewelers, even in a day when jewels for royal families were considered necessities for maintaining their prestige and station in life.

In Russia, the royal family was headed for a revolution that would spread across their nation like wild rot—and destroy them in the process. But in the early morning hours of the many Easter Sundays which preceded the chaos of the Revolution, war and bloodshed were not even thought of; and each Easter Sunday was begun with a presentation of the royal eggs.

Each Easter morning the Czar himself presented a royal egg to the Czarina, and an equally beautiful egg was presented to the Dowager Empress. Altogether there were fifty-seven imperial Easter eggs made and presented to the royal family. Today these eggs are valued at $5,000,000.

The exact date the first imperial egg was made is not known, but

it was probably in 1884. The eggs were fine and masterful examples
of the best art in Russia. The shells were decorated on the outside
with pearls, diamonds and rubies. Opening of the shells revealed
the eggs' inner secrets: miniature crowns and rings, picture frames,
and platinum swans; golden rosebuds and miniature ruby eggs. One
of these eggs even held within it a small train, perfect in every detail.

Yet the art of Fabergé was swept along on the tides of the Revolution. When chaos struck, refugees from all walks of life sold everything they could to gather enough money to get away from the at-
tacking horde. What they could not sell and what was not lost, the
Soviets claimed for themselves.

A custom begun by Alexander III in an attempt to cheer up his
wife, and later continued by Nicholas II—who gave two eggs a year,
one to his wife and one to Alexander III's widow—thus ended in
Revolution. Fabergé himself was finished in Russia.

His work, however, remains. Most of the imperial eggs have been
preserved in collections both in Russia and in England. Yet there
are some that are missing. There are four of these fabulous eggs
which were lost in the chaos of Revolution—and they have never
been found.

THE first of these missing eggs is the Danish Silver Jubilee Egg,
which was presented to Marie Feodorovna by Alexander III in
the year 1888. Since the egg was made in celebration of the Silver
Jubilee of the King of Denmark, its design was in keeping with the
occasion.

A white and pale blue egg, encrusted with precious gems, a dia-
mond-set fillet, a diamond monogram and carved golden masks, it
is topped with a Danish royal elephant and supported by three of
the Danish heraldic lions.

When the egg was opened, it revealed a two-sided portrait screen
topped by diamonds, crowns and initials. The screen holds two
portraits, one of King Christian of Denmark and one of Queen Lou-
ise of Denmark. Approximately ten inches high, this egg is surely
one of the most fantastic of the world's missing treasures.

The first egg ever presented to Alexandra Feodorovna is among
the missing eggs. Much smaller than the Danish Silver Jubilee Egg,
it is only three inches high, made of engraved gold, translucent

strawberry reds and opaque white enamels; it sports gold mounts and Cupid's arrows set with rose diamonds. The date of the gift of the egg (1895) is clearly inscribed on the base immediately below a rose diamond. On the top of the egg is a portrait of Nicholas II.

When the egg is opened, the first item you will see will be a golden rosebud; yet, after removing the rosebud from the egg, you will discover another item within the rosebud: an imperial crown of rubies and diamonds. But even then the treasures are not exhausted, for within the crown itself will be found a miniature ruby egg.

Certainly, this second of the lost eggs, known as the "Rosebud Egg," is one of the most beautiful of the missing treasures of the world.

Inside the third missing egg is a platinum swan which, when wound up, wags its tail, moves along a certain course and raises and lowers its head. As a final touch, the wings themselves open and each platinum feather is seen distinctly.

The swan sits on a lake which is nothing less than a single aquamarine. Water lilies, in four colors of gold, decorate the lake as well as the handle which lifts the swan and his lake from the egg. The outside of the golden egg is mat enameled mauve, decorated with a rose diamond trellis, and at the top as well as the bottom of the egg will be found single, large, portrait diamonds.

Presented to Alexandra Feodorovna by Nicholas II in 1906, and only four inches high, this so-called "Swan Egg" is the third and one of the most beautiful of the missing imperial eggs.

The last of the missing eggs is appropriately called the "Egg with Love Trophies," since it contains a miniature picture frame which, in a lovely design of enamel and diamonds, forms a heart.

In keeping with the Love Trophy theme of the egg, the strut of the frame forms the signature NIKI since it was a gift from Nicholas II to Alexandra Feodorovna. It was Nicholas' portrait which was in the heart-shaped frame.

On the top of the outside of the egg is a basket of roses made of rose diamonds, gold, pearls, enamels and rubies. At the base of the egg are four quivers, and peeping out of these are arrow-top set diamonds. The body of the egg is gold enameled with pale blue. The decorations are carved gold and white enamel bands.

The date of the creation of this egg is not known, but it was probably either 1910 or 1911, and only the approximate measurement of the egg is known. It is thought that the entire egg stands nine inches high while the picture frame is approximately three and one half inches high.

Yet, whether the actual measurements are known or not, this egg with its lovely "love trophies" could never be mistaken for anything but what it is: a fortune in the form of one of the most fantastic Easter eggs ever created.

Any of these missing eggs are worth a fortune—if you can find them.

Yet these are not the only things Fabergé made that are missing, including Easter eggs which were smaller than the imperial eggs and which were made for the families of the nobility. These were small, jeweled eggs which were designed to be worn on long chains as necklaces.

Fabergé made many things, all of them exquisite. He made cigarette cases and clocks, and miniature animals and items for milady's dressing table. He made tie pins and cuff links, and crosses—and all of them collectors' items—if you can find one of them.

They would not have, of course, the value of one of the imperial Easter eggs but, certainly, they would be worth a great deal. Anything by Fabergé is worth something—and the imperial eggs are worth the most of all—if you can find them.

But even the lowly, everyday eggshell merely decorated for Easter can be worth a fortune—if you know one when you see it.

Not too many years ago an eggshell was sold for twenty-five thousand gold francs, but it was not just any eggshell. It was a rare egg painted by a master craftsman. There was a time when such artists as Watteau, Lancret and Boucher painted eggshells for Easter. Not always of a religious nature, yet they were gay eggs painted for the Easter season. And today they would be worth a small fortune—if you can find them.

See color plate
II. Top: "Orange Tree Egg" by Fabergé, presented to Dowager Empress Marie Feodorovna by Nicholas II, dated 1911. Based on solid block of nephrite, surrounded by four gold-mounted nephrite posts connected by swinging chains of translucent emerald enameled gold leaves, half covering pearls. Egg-shaped nephrite leaves enclose a feathered gold bird which—when a small button is pressed—rises from the interior, sings, and automatically disappears. Bottom: "Jeweled 1894 Easter Egg" by Fabergé, presented to Marie Feodorovna by Alexander III. Carved from a block of agate, it forms a jewel casket. The year is made of diamonds. Carved gold lions' heads are mounted at each end.
Courtesy of A LA VIEILLE RUSSIE, N.Y.

II

LINCOLNIANA

Treasures from the Time of Abraham Lincoln

THERE is a missing letter which is worth $100,000 if you can find it.

On November 21, 1864, the *Boston Transcript* published an appeal to the general public, an appeal which was in the very finest newspaper tradition.

A widow needed help, and the paper was asking the general public to acknowledge her need. In sorrowful terms the *Boston Transcript* told the story of a woman who, before the advent of the war between the states, had had five sons. Now those sons were dead— dead on the field of battle in defense of the Union.

The newspaper cried out for her, begging the people for their sympathy and their help in this, her time of need. Throughout the nation, people read the story and felt sorry for the grieving mother.

One person in particular read the story and felt deep sorrow because of it. This reader wrote a letter to the widow, telling her of his sympathy. In due time the letter was delivered to the widow, and, when she opened it, this is what she read:

Executive Mansion,

Washington, Nov. 21, 1864

To Mrs. Bixby, Boston, Mass.

Dear Madam: I have been shown in the files of the War Department a statement of the Adjutant General of Massachusetts that you are the mother of five sons who have died gloriously on the field of battle.

7

I feel how weak and fruitless must be any words of mine which should attempt to beguile you for the grief of a loss so overwhelming. But I cannot refrain from tendering to you the consolation that may be found in the thanks of the Republic they died to save.

I pray that our Heavenly Father may assuage the anguish of your bereavement, and leave you only the cherished memory of the loved and lost, and the solemn pride that must be yours, to have laid so costly a sacrifice upon the altar of freedom.

Yours, very sincerely and respectfully,

A. Lincoln

Mrs. Bixby

Today, the original of that letter which the widow opened and read such a long time ago would be worth $100,000—if you could find it.

The ironic part of the whole episode of that letter is that Lincoln had been completely misled in his understanding of the situation. Mrs. Bixby's five sons were *not* killed on the battlefield, although it is true that two of them did die in battle; but there were also two sons who, instead of dying "gloriously on the field of battle," ignominiously deserted their army and their cause. Neither did the fifth son die in battle, yet he, at least, did not desert. Rather, he was honorably discharged.

On November 21, there had been the plea for Mrs. Bixby in the *Boston Transcript,* written by Adjutant General William Schouler. Lincoln had already had information about the widow at the time this item was printed, but on publication of the appeal Lincoln wrote to Schouler for additional details. With all of this, it seems rather amazing that there should have been such a mistake made, although it was certainly not Mr. Lincoln's mistake, but rather the mistakes of those around him.

But the ironic fact that the letter which Lincoln wrote was composed in error certainly does not detract either from the historical, moral or monetary value of the letter. The beauty of the letter will remain forever, and the monetary value of the letter today stands at $100,000. Yet, can you find it?

Where it is now, nobody knows. We do know that Lincoln himself did not mail the letter, because he did not have Mrs. Bixby's address. He gave it to Schouler, who had it delivered.

It would seem then that the letter disappeared almost immediately after Mrs. Bixby received it. Members of her family seemed to feel that she did not have the letter at the time of her death in 1878.

Today no one knows where it could be; but the value of the letter was apparent almost immediately. Facsimiles and forgeries, both, have flooded the country time after time.

As early as 1891, one man with an eye for business, Tobin by name, registered an engraving of the Lincoln letter with the Librarian of Congress on April 25, 1891. He called it "Lincoln's Letter" and sold copies for $2 apiece—in a day when $2 went a lot further than it does today.

Sometimes, today, these old facsimiles are found, and thought, with all honest intentions, by hopeful treasure hunters, to be the original. They are, of course, disappointed to find they have what is only a facsimile. Yet the search continues for the original letter.

The story of this letter is filled with legends like the one that the original of the Bixby letter is in the Library of Congress, but unfortunately (or rather fortunately for the treasure hunter) this is not so.

The original was, also, at one time supposed to be on exhibit at Huber's Museum in New York City—at least according to a copy of said "original" put out by Huber himself.

It has also been reported that the original letter was in the J. Pierpont Morgan collection, but the Morgan family reported that they knew nothing about the letter.

Many, many times it has been said that the Bostonian Society had the original, but the society has denied this emphatically.

The letter may have been destroyed—and if it has been then it is lost to the treasure hunter. Yet, I do not think so. As stated above, many forgeries and many honest facsimiles have been made. Copies of the letter were printed in the daily newspapers less than a week after Mrs. Bixby received the original.

It must be true, then, that somewhere along the line—at a time when the value of the letter was already apparent—that the original was in hands other than the Widow Bixby's. Otherwise where did the copies come from? You must have an original from which to make a copy. Somewhere along the line someone had the original and from that he made the first copies.

With luck, that original letter is still in existence, and you can trade it for $100,000—if you can find it.

IF you can find an autograph copy of the Gettysburg Address, you can almost name your own price for it. One copy known to be authentic sold for $54,000.

This is the speech which is common knowledge to every schoolboy. Any child can begin this famous oration, which begins with "Four score and seven years ago . . ."

The Address, which was given on November 19, 1863, was spoken at the dedication of the battleground of Gettysburg, a national cemetery.

There are known, today, to be in existence five copies of the Gettysburg Address. The five extant papers include Lincoln's first draft, the reading text, and the revised copies made up after the speech had been delivered.

Yet besides these known copies are the stories of yet another copy —a copy which has never been found. This missing version of the speech was an autograph copy which was made up for Judge David Mills and was evidently written the night before the Gettysburg dedication ceremony, since Lincoln stayed at Mills' home as a guest on that night.

No one knows where that copy is now, but if you can find it you can almost name your own price for it—perhaps even as high as the aforementioned $54,000.

Yet there are other things which belonged to Lincoln which today are missing—and which can be of value to the treasure hunter.

The sport of hunting for missing Lincolniana heightens in furor year by year. The admirers of Lincoln increase by the thousands as each year passes, as they seek more information and more facts concerning the man who was probably America's greatest statesman. Accordingly they also increase their desire for the things which he owned, used or touched.

There was a pen which Lincoln allegedly had in his possession on the night he died. Today, no one knows where it is.

Originally, the pen had been one of a pair which had been presented to Lincoln at the time of his inauguration, but the penholders have a far older history than that. In a much earlier time there had been a desk which belonged to the captain of the Mayflower. Later the lid of that desk was made into a carved chest which held surveying instruments, and that chest was presented to George Washington. Then, in turn, the box was made over into the pair of penholders.

Lincoln presented one of these pens to a Mr. Isaac Reed, and he promised Mr. Reed that he would forward to him papers showing the authenticity of the pen—but three days later Lincoln was murdered. The papers had been filled out but were lost in the confusion of Lincoln's death.

Reed treasured his Lincoln pen and took it all over the world with him, asking various people to use it as they signed their autographs for him. One of those who did so, using this famous pen, was Queen Victoria of England.

The other pen was the one which was allegedly in Lincoln's possession the night he died. As to the value of this pen, if it could be found, there is no way of telling, without of course finding it and holding it for auction. At one time, Reed had the opportunity to sell the pen he owned for three hundred English pounds—quite a sum in those days.

Pens, of course, are not the only missing items of Lincoln. Even his watches are cause for diligent search. On many occasions Lincoln was presented with watches, a common form of official and semi-official gift in those days. Not all of these watches have been found—and they are well worth looking for.

Even his hats are items of value, but not in the way it might seem. While it is true that Lincoln hats are collectors' items, it must also be remembered that Lincoln used his famous stovepipe hats for convenient storage places. In these hats he put papers of all kinds—from items relating to his law practice to official state documents. Almost anything, and possibly something of great value, might be found in one of these old hats.

Collectors ask for such items of wearing apparel as boots, socks, gloves, coats, and even his nightgowns. These items of course are not of great value, yet they are worth enough to have them checked by an expert.

Even Lincoln canes, rings and cuff buttons are sought. This Lincolniana frenzy extends even to items belonging to members of the Lincoln family. There is the story of Mrs. Lincoln's garnets—although this is a story which, heard many years ago, this author has been unable to verify.

It is the story of Mrs. Lincoln's need for hard cash and, like many other American women, she sold her jewels to raise some money—in this case a set of garnets.

Although this story may not be true, Mrs. Lincoln did like jewelry. Tiffany's in New York, for example, made for her a matching set of seed-pearl earrings and necklace to be worn at her husband's Second Inaugural.

Tiffany's today no longer has any records of the seed pearls, although, according to Mr. Wm. J. Fielding of Tiffany's, ". . . understand some of the institutions in Washington, D.C. have some of these pieces and photographs of them."

Garnets, powder horns and wallets! The mania for Lincolniana extends even to their furniture. Furniture from both the White House and the Springfield house are sought by collectors, with particular attention given to chairs, since the chairs of the family seem to carry more interest than other items of furniture.

Among the chairs associated with the Lincolns, and which are known to be missing, are a tall, hall chair and a set of plain, wooden chairs which had flowers painted on their backs. Chairs also worth watching for are those which Lincoln used in his law practice, because they seem to have a special appeal to collectors.

The value of a Lincoln chair is difficult to judge, since each item would of necessity be of different condition and make. Also the price of the item would vary according to how much part the chair had played in the history of the nation. For example, a chair which Lincoln had used at the time of a great historic event would be of far more value than just any chair which he had used.

However, I have seen prices ranging from $100 to $250 per chair.

Chairs, hats, canes, or whatever, there is a chance of finding them —all except one item which is probably the strangest of all lost Lincolniana: an entire log cabin.

"Log cabin" is synonymous with the very name of Lincoln, and in 1830 when Lincoln's family moved to Illinois, Abraham pitched in to help clear the land, fence the property, and build the inevitable log cabin.

Years later, in 1865, this cabin was an item of much public interest when it was displayed as an exhibit of the Chicago Sanitary Fair. Following this exhibition, the log cabin was shown at Barnum's Museum in New York City. Eventually the cabin was loaded aboard a ship so that it could be exhibited in England. But the ship was lost at sea, carrying with it a piece of Lincolniana which can never be replaced. Surely, this must be the strangest of the lost Lincolniana.

The more everyday items belonging to Lincoln are, however, quite within the scope of today's treasure hunter, from the very valuable missing autograph copy of the Gettysburg Address to the satchels which he carried. Anything which he owned or used is worth checking—of course, being careful that you have all the proper facts.

Do not, above all, be like the person who tried to sell a piece of rail which he claimed Lincoln had split while he was still living on the family farm in Kentucky. He "forgot" the fact that when the Lincoln family left the Kentucky farm, "Little Abe" was only two years old—and not even Abraham Lincoln rated the title of a two-year-old rail splitter.

But if you have anything at all which belonged to the Lincoln family, have it checked. It is bound to be worth something.

III

THEIR PENS WERE DIPPED IN GOLD

Autographs and Historical Letters

ACRIPPLED artist found an old piece of paper—and sold it for $51,000. Not because it was just any piece of paper, but because scrawled across it was the most famous signature in the world, the signature of Button Gwinnett.

To most people, the name Gwinnett simply means another signer of the Declaration of Independence, but to autograph collectors, the signature is the one most famous and most rare in all the world, so rare that the price paid for a Gwinnett keeps going up and up, and the end is nowhere in sight.

Over a comparatively short number of years the price of a Gwinnett signature has gone from a little over $4,000 to over $50,000 and, as the years go on, the autograph will become even more rare—and the price will continue to rise.

One reason that the Gwinnett is so sought after is the fact that autograph collectors prize greatly a complete set of the signers of the Declaration of Independence, and it is the Button Gwinnett signature which most of them lack, because it is so rarely found.

Yet there are other collections which the autograph hound seeks diligently, and among these sets are those of the signers of the Constitution. A complete set of autograph letters of the signers is valued at approximately $25,000.

Single examples of the autographs of the signers of the Constitution can also bring fabulous prices—such as the autograph of Thomas Lynch, which has been known to bring $5,000 to the seller.

Prices vary, of course, on most autographs, since this is a collectors' market and in most cases the price a signature will bring in the open market or in an auction depends on the demand, yet, often, if the autograph is rare enough and the specimen is good, the value soars out of sight.

Rare autographs can be hidden away anywhere, waiting for you to find them. In an old trunk in your attic, tied up in a perfumed array of old love letters, hidden between the pages of a book; hidden almost any place small enough for a piece of paper, a letter or an old bill to remain unseen for a day, a month or a year; hidden until such time as the treasure hunter happens across it.

Most important, of course, in a search of this type is knowing which autographs are rare and valuable. There are those that are important because they are Americana and rare—and dear to us because they represent a part of our history—such as Gwinnett and Lynch. There are others, also rare and also sought after, such as Morton and Middleton, and Heywood and Hart.

FROM other nations, too, come autographs of vast importance to the treasure hunter, and one of these is the signature of Sir Francis Drake. Any scrap of paper, any book, anything upon which this great Englishman signed his name is worth checking by the treasure hunter, because the autograph of Sir Francis Drake is one of the most highly prized autographs in the world.

Also from England comes the signature of the blind poet, John Milton. His autograph, sought by collectors all over the world, is considered rare. It is ironic that this man, who sold his greatest work, *Paradise Lost,* for a measly $50, is today not only respected for his great poetry, but for his signature, which he undoubtedly scrawled on many papers—his letters, his daily notes, his memos on the state of the Puritans of Cromwell's England.

And where are the autographs of Milton? They could be anywhere. Autographs are found in the oddest places and are passed over year after year because the average person does not recognize them for what they are.

One of these unsung autographs might well be that of Sir Thomas

More, who lived during the time of Henry VIII. Thomas More was the statesman who dreamed of a better life and told about it in *Utopia*. He told of a land where all men were equal, both in labor and rights, and every man was respected and human dignity inherent. Today, just his autograph would satisfy the treasure hunter, because it is one of the highest priced in the autograph field.

There was also, in a later time, another historically important figure whose name, today, cries out for recognition to all hunters of lost treasure because her signature has become one of the most highly prized autographs of all time. Yet, within her own lifetime, when her name was set to paper by her own hand, it was unknown —even to the man she murdered.

She sent two letters to Jean Paul Marat, the fanatic who led the people of France through a revolutionary blood bath that even now stains the memory of the glory of France.

Not knowing who she was, Marat at first refused her admittance, and when he finally did allow her to enter his room, he was in the bathtub. She sat quite close to him and watched him as he bathed. Hidden in her scarf was a dagger.

She spoke softly to him, telling him only the things he wanted to hear, promising him a new list of names of royalists for the guillotine. He listened quietly, not noticing that she moved closer and closer as she spoke. When she was quite close to him she stabbed him.

For this "crime" she was guillotined, and of her courage even her enemies said, "She has killed us, but she teaches us how to die."

This woman who killed so justly and died so bravely was named Charlotte (de) Corday. It is this signature that we must remember, yet we must also keep in mind that she was born Marie Anne Charlotte Corday d'Armans, and her signature may be written either way. There quite probably would be a difference in value in the two signatures, because, while they are the same woman, it is as Charlotte Corday that she became famous.

Also, of course, in any history of autographs, the practitioners of the arts cannot be forgotten. A man of music, the younger Bach left signatures which are highly sought.

In the world of art the autograph probably most highly regarded is that of a young man who lived in the 1500s, a man who had many names, and who is remembered by his people for many things.

Even in his own lifetime he was loved by the people of Italy, and today they remember him as the son of a painter and poet, from a place called Urbino which was nothing more than a hill, bleak and isolated in the midst of desolate mountains.

They remember him as the young pupil of Perugino, of Perugia, where he painted his first pictures. They remember him as the youth who listened enraptured to the rumors in the air, fantastic rumors of two painters from Florence. Unusual painters, these, for one painted with his left hand and one gazed at his work over the bridge of a crooked and broken nose.

And when the young man went to Florence to see for himself the left-handed da Vinci and his competitor, the broken-nosed Michelangelo, the Florentines called him the "Youthful Master."

Today not only his countrymen but all the world remember him for the art he produced: the "Disputa del Sacramento," the "School of Athens," the unsurpassable "Jurisprudence," and many others—altogether over two hundred of the world's greatest paintings.

Yet the searcher for lost autographs is not interested, primarily, in the works of art which this man produced nor in what he was called—still, it is a strange thing that he was known by many names.

His last name was Sanzio, but it was also written Santi. The Italians who loved him called him Raffaelle. They also called him Raffaello. But his paintings as well as his writings he signed merely: Raphael.

Raphael, More, Corday, Gwinnett, Lynch, and so on down the list of fabulous autographs, whatever the signature, it is there waiting to make a fortune for you—if you can find it.

A LETTER written by Ulysses S. Grant sold for $910—yet the usual price for a Grant letter is around $10.

Two letters written by Abraham Lincoln brought over $1,000 at auction—yet the usual Lincoln letter is only worth a couple of hundred dollars.

A letter by George Washington could bring as high as $1,000—yet a Washington letter is usually worth only about $100.

Why? What is there about a certain letter, a certain scrawled memo, a certain written word, that raises its value out of the ordinary?

In the case of the Grant letter, Ulysses S. Grant, as a dutiful son, was informing his father that he was joining the United States Army.

The letters by Lincoln were not just any letters. They were letters that were of historical importance to our nation. Lincoln was writing of history as it was being made.

A letter by Washington could bring $1,000 if it spoke of the actions of his colleagues, the events of the war with England, or any other historical episode of his period.

It is the historical value of such letters as these which raises their value. Their contents speak of times and things which are past; yet, if we can read about them in the handwriting of the men who actually lived them, how much more vivid these times are to us.

These letters of historical significance are always important items to watch for. Many times there are little-known or forgotten episodes or whole periods of history which have been told in the form of correspondence between one friend and another.

Imagine the value of a letter from Washington which might read, "Tonight I am going to cross the Delaware." Or a letter from Lincoln which might read, "Tomorrow I am going to free the slaves." These letters, of course, are purely imaginary; yet, letters of equal historical importance have been found in the past, and will be found again by some lucky treasure hunter who just happens to look in the right place at the right time.

There will be letters found which are similar in historical significance. Today there are already many examples of letters of this type in the museums of the nation and in the hands of the collectors, letters telling of history as it happened.

The Spanish text of a unique historical letter is now owned by the New York Public Library. This letter is probably one of the most important in the world as regards historical content, for it was in this letter that Christopher Columbus announced that he had discovered a new world.

Letters have been found from all sorts of people. Letters by Mary Lincoln have been found, speaking of the episodes of her husband's life, his times, his political and spiritual ideals.

There is a letter written by Americus Vespucius to his father, which is now in the British Museum.

ILLUSTRATIONS

1 to 9

1. An Imperial Easter Egg by Fabergé, about 1903. The egg, clock and stand are of red and green gold, translucent and opaque blue enamel and opalescent white enamel, and pearls. The egg was probably presented to the Dowager Empress Marie Feodorovna in 1903 by her son, Tzar Nicholas II. Each hour is announced by a chanticleer which rises from the interior, crowing and flapping its wings. *(Ch. I)*

Four score and seven years ago our fathers brought forth upon this continent, a new nation, conceived in Liberty, and dedicated to the proposition that all men are created equal.

Now we are engaged in a great civil war, testing whether that nation, or any nation so conceived, and so dedicated, can long endure. We are met on a great battle-field of that war. We have come to dedicate a portion of that field, as a final resting place for those who here gave their lives, that that nation might live. It is altogether fitting and proper that we should do this.

But, in a larger sense, we can not dedicate— we can not consecrate— we can not hallow— this ground. The brave men, living and dead, who struggled here, have consecrated it, far above our poor power to add or detract. The world will little note, nor long remember, what we say here, but it can never forget what they did here. It is for us the living, rather, to be dedicated here to the unfinished work which they who fought here, have, thus far, so nobly advanced. It is rather for us to be here dedicated to the great task remaining before us— that from these honored dead we take increased devotion to that cause for which they here gave the last full measure of devotion— that we here highly resolve that these dead shall not have died in vain— that this nation, under God, shall have a new birth of freedom— and that, government of the people, by the people, for the people, shall not perish from the earth.

2. A copy of the above Gettysburg Address in Abraham Lincoln's handwriting sold for $54,000; one autographed copy is still missing. (Ch. II)

Courtesy of the Illinois State Historical Society

3. This is the signature of Button Gwinnett, one of the signers of the Declaration of Independence. His autograph sold for over $50,000 at a recent sale. (*Ch. III*)

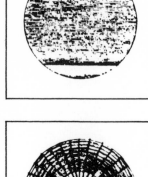

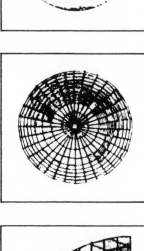

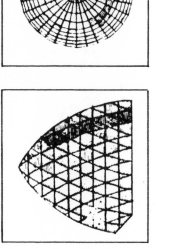

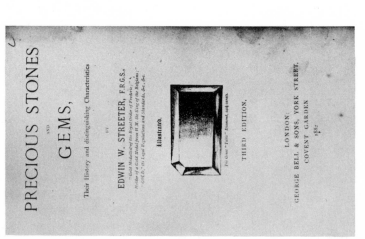

4. Left: drawing of the Great Table Diamond, 242 carats. A fortune awaits its finder. 5. Right: side, top and bottom views of the Great Mogul Diamond—another missing gem. Some authorities believe that the Mogul is really the Orloff (bottom right), a 199-carat diamond, now reposing in the Diamond Room in the Kremlin. (Ch. IV)

PRECIOUS STONES
AND
GEMS,

Their History and distinguishing Characteristics

BY

EDWIN W. STREETER, F.R.G.S.,

"Gold Medallist for Royal Order of Frederic";
Holder of a Gold Medal from H. M. the King of the Belgians;
"GOLD," its Legal Regulations and Standards, &c., &c.

Illustrated.

The Great "Table" Diamond, 242 carats.

THIRD EDITION.

LONDON:
GEORGE BELL & SONS, YORK STREET,
COVENT GARDEN
1882

22

6. These buttons are collectors' items. Shown here are rare buttons with fans and hands in interesting designs. (*Ch. V*)

Courtesy of Hobbies, The Magazine for Collectors

7. Buttons of all kinds have long been a favorite of collectors. Here, some fine examples of various kinds of fruit on buttons. *(Ch. V)*

Courtesy of Hobbies, The Magazine for Collectors

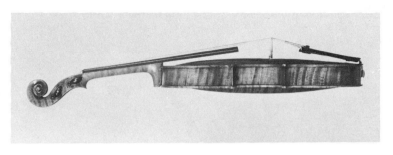

8. Front, rear and side view of a Stradivarius violin. In good condition, these instruments are worth a small fortune—if you can find one. *(Ch. VI)*

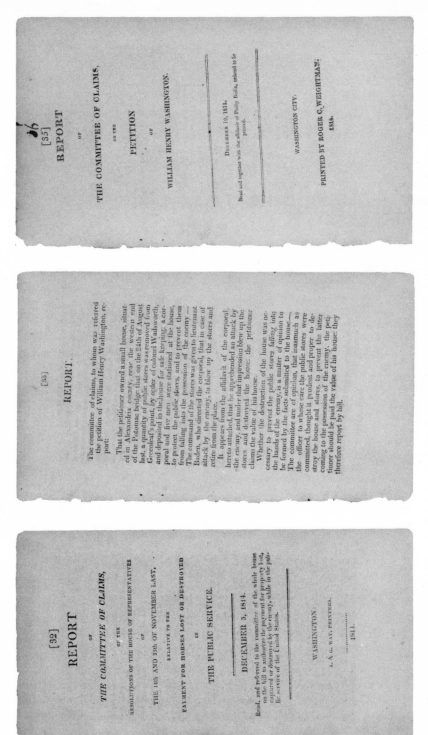

9. Printed copies of American records of the War of 1812. Note the date, December 1814, four months after the burning of the city of Washington by British troops. (*Ch. VII*)

Not all of the famous letters have been found, however. There are letters which we do not even know exist—letters which will remain undiscovered until the lucky treasure hunter finds them hidden away in old trunks and attics or slipped between the pages of a book.

Historical importance, however, is not the only thing which can raise the value of the handwritten word. Many other factors must also be taken into consideration.

A second-hand copy of Beale's *History of the Sperm Whale* sold for $2,200—yet a second-hand copy of the same book is usually worth only about a dime.

This second-hand copy of Beale's *History of the Sperm Whale* was on the face of it certainly worth only a dime, but scrawled across its pages were notes made by an author who was using this copy of the book as a textbook for a novel that was to become a classic.

The author was Herman Melville; the novel was *Moby Dick.*

The book of itself was worthless, but the working notes of a master novelist made it of value.

Notes by famous authors on their works, marginal notes on documents, notations, and memos may all be of value—if they are in some way related to a great event, a great person, or a great work, and if they are in the handwriting of a famous person.

One other missive which should not be overlooked is the love letter. A packet of love letters from the famous people of another day can be of great value to the lucky finder.

Diaries must also be kept on the treasure hunter's list. Many men and women have kept diaries, from some of which we may glean an insight into the past.

There are missing diaries written by men and women who lived during exciting periods of history. These diaries would be invaluable—if you could find them.

Watch for letters, diaries, notes, and memos written during periods of revolution or war. Look for items penned during any of the periods of great upheaval in the world's history. Make sure that they are written by famous people or written by someone who knew and associated with the famous.

Watch for these writings in second-hand stores, in junk shops, and at auctions. Search for them in the attics and cellars of old houses.

Old books are a common hiding place for letters—either tucked between the pages or in the binding. Or sometimes, as in the case of Herman Melville and Beale's *History of the Sperm Whale,* the valuable notations are right on the pages of the book itself.

If it is handwritten, and important enough, you can trade a book, a packet of yellowed letters, or a forgotten memo for a fortune.

IV

Royal Baubles

Fabulous Precious Stones

IN the seventeenth century, the official buyer of gems for the King of France traveled to the court of Aurangzeb in India, where he saw three of the greatest diamonds the world has ever known.

One of these diamonds was of a lovely blue shade, weighing one hundred and twelve carats. The second resembled a gum drop in shape and weighed two hundred and eighty carats. The last was shaped very much like the top of a miniature table and weighed two hundred and forty-two carats.

One of these diamonds disappeared during a bloody revolution. The other, we think, was a part of the booty taken by Nadir Shah. And the third simply disappeared. Three of the world's greatest diamonds, yet two of them have never been found. Only one has ever reappeared, however, in different form. Fortunately for the treasure hunter, the hunt is still wide open for two of them.

The above buyer of gems, Jean Baptiste Tavernier, immediately knew when he saw the first of the three diamonds that it was the only one of its kind that had ever been found. It was a unique shade of blue, and, though it weighed over one hundred carats, it was the gem's color that impressed him the most. No man had ever before found a diamond of that particular shade, and to this day that statement is still true.

Tavernier bought the diamond, and, for the sake of faceting and beauty, had the stone reduced in size to sixty-seven and one-eighth carats. He then sold the diamond, now named the Tavernier Blue, to his King, Louis XIV of France. It is said that Louis suspended the diamond from a light blue ribbon and wore it around his neck.

The diamond then was safe—until the outbreak of the French Revolution. When, at that time, a part of the valuables of the royal family of France were taken and placed in the *Garde Meubles* (furniture repository), they found that the diamond had disappeared.

Its whereabouts remained unknown, until one day thirty-two years later a gem dealer listed a stone for sale which was the exact shade of the Tavernier Blue, although it was smaller than the original diamond. Later, two other smaller stones were also offered for sale, both of them of the identical shade.

Coincidence would not explain the similarity of coloring of these stones to the blue diamond. Nor would coincidence explain the fact that the three stones offered for sale would, if placed together and allowances made for loss of weight in cleavage and cutting, exactly match the size and shape of the large blue diamond.

The larger of these stones is today one of the most famous diamonds in the world, and also one of the greatest "finds" in the history of treasure hunting.

We do not know this stone today as the Tavernier Blue. It has a new history now, a new name, and weighs forty-four carats. It is called the Hope diamond. It is now part of a collection in the Smithsonian Museum, in Washington, D.C.

The second diamond Tavernier saw was the gum drop diamond, the Great Mogul. At the time he viewed it, the diamond weighed two hundred and eighty carats—yet originally it had weighed more than twice this amount, seven hundred and eighty-seven carats.

Magnificent in its great size, it was cut down to a mere two hundred and eighty carats by a Venetian gem cutter who lived to regret his butchering of the great stone.

Hortensio Berghis was the diamond cutter who botched the job, and instead of being paid for his work he was fined ten thousand rupees for the vandalism he had done to the great stone.

Yet certainly a diamond that weighs two hundred and eighty carats is still worth the treasure hunters' while, for the Great Mogul is still missing—one of the greatest lost treasures of all time.

It disappeared shortly after Tavernier saw it. This magnificent lost stone has been described as a rose-cut diamond, round and a little high on one side, like a gum drop with facets. It was "flat" underneath and the top was faceted. This is the typical rose cut.

It has been suggested (as always there are suggestions of this type in the case of lost gems) that the Great Mogul was cut down into one of two other stones, e.g., either the Koh-i-noor or the Orlov diamond. Yet the Koh-i-noor and the Orlov both have histories of their own.

There is a legend that the Koh-i-noor diamond is five thousand years old and is one of those stones which has been followed by the curse of bloodshed and tribulation.

It has been the loot of wars. One ruler let himself be blinded rather than give it up. At one time it was hidden in the plaster of a prison cell and then rediscovered accidentally.

Nadir Shah, a man of low birth but of great ambition and such cruelty that his own officers finally killed him, sacked Delhi, India, and took, among other things, the Koh-i-noor diamond. Finally, however, the East India Company became the owners of the Koh-i-noor, and they presented it to Queen Victoria in 1849.

The Orlov diamond, which has been claimed by some to be the cut-down version of the Great Mogul, has a history that could have come straight out of Hollywood.

How many movies have you seen where a diamond was stolen from its resting place in the eye of a heathen idol? Probably a great many and, probably, they were most of them based on the story of the Orlov, which originally did rest in the eye of an idol. Later it, too, like the Koh-i-noor, became a part of the booty of Nadir Shah.

The stone, under two hundred carats, was purchased finally by Count Grigori Orlov, and in the latter part of the eighteenth century Prince Orlov presented the diamond to Catherine II of Russia. It became a part of the Russian crown jewels, being set in the royal sceptre.

The Koh-i-noor and the Orlov both have fantastic histories of their own. It does not seem possible that either of them could be what is left of the Great Mogul, the stone that was in every way worthy of the name it bore. Associated with the Great Mogul are names right out of an Arabian fairy tale. Baber, who founded the Mogul Dynasty! Hindustan! Shah Jehan, the fifth to succeed Baber!

Shah Jehan was called the Great Mogul, and the great diamond was his namesake. This was the same Shah Jehan who built the Taj Mahal and the $30,000,000 Peacock Throne; yet even the Great

Mogul found misfortune in his life. Shah Jehan became ill, and his son, Aurangzeb, seized him and imprisoned him for the rest of his life. Aurangzeb was the last of the Great Moguls.

The Aurangzeb whom Tavernier visited was a scholar and a man of abstinence who abstained from dancing, singing, and meat. He drank nothing but water. Such was the man who owned the Great Mogul, one of the largest diamonds in the world, a diamond which has disappeared, a diamond which is waiting to be found by a lucky treasure hunter—in an antique shop, a trunk in some cellar, or a second-hand store.

The third diamond Tavernier saw was the Great Table diamond, weighing two hundred and forty-two carats. The actual weight of this stone, however, is two hundred and forty-two and five-sixteenths carats, or 249.46 metric carats, although in a stone of this size the exact weight is unimportant. Anything over two hundred carats is well worth looking for.

Like the Great Mogul, the Great Table diamond has disappeared. Can't you picture yourself as being the one to find a long, flat stone faintly resembling in design the flat top of a table and weighing over two hundred carats? You would need to find this kind of "junk" only once.

Tavernier saw three diamonds. First there was the Great Mogul —and it disappeared. Then there was the Great Table—and it disappeared. And then there was one, the fabulous Hope diamond, the only one left out of three of the most fantastic gems the world has ever seen.

HALFWAY around the world in a land called Kandy there was a gem stone so rare that only one of its kind had ever been found. Today, that is still true. There has never been another gem stone like it ever formed in the earth; at least not a perfect, flawless stone like this one.

In the early 1800's, Kandy was still the land of temple bells, Sanskrit manuscripts and Oriental mystery. Located on the island of Ceylon, it was a place of romance and eastern lore—and also the location of the gem that is so rare that even today most jewelers will deny it ever existed at all.

The gem was a spinel, and, although there are many, many spinels in existence, all the rest are colored. This one is white, and it is unique. There has never been another flawless, white spinel discovered. It weighs seventy-one and a quarter carats—and it is missing. It is probably the most unique lost treasure in the gem field, for there is only one like it.

It is almost impossible to estimate the value of such a stone without holding it up for auction or having various authorities quote their prices and then taking the best one. Yet at one time a value of £23,000 was placed on this gem—and that was many years ago. Today, the value would be far more, perhaps a million dollars!

The first time the white spinel of Kandy was heard of was in the year 1803. At that time Boldoc Swamie, the King of Kandy, presented Major Robert Honner of H.M. 19th Regiment of Foot with the fabulous stone.

It is supposed that the presentation of such a fabulous gift was occasioned by certain distinguished services on the part of the British Major Honner. Yet there are no official records of this gift or the reasons for its presentation, probably because the gift was personal rather than official.

What we do know of the stone is that it was set in gold and surrounded by rubies, an impressive and beautiful sight. Though Major Honner must have been very proud of his fantastic gem, there came a time when he offered the gem for sale. Not even his pride in the gift of the King of Kandy would allow him to keep it. The reason? His military record from the Public Record Office in England speaks for itself:

Major Robert Honner—19th Regiment of Foot (Army Lists and General Courts Martial—Confirmed at Home, W.O. 92/1)

25 January 1792—Ensign in the 19th Regiment of Foot
16 September 1792—Lieutenant
27 May 1793—Captain
18 April 1805—Major
30 January 1806—Court-martialled in Ceylon for violent conduct in the mess-room. Sentenced to be cashiered from the Army but he was permitted to sell his commission for the support of his wife and family.

It is obvious that for monetary reasons Major Honner had to sell the white gem. He needed money so badly that after his court-martial he was permitted to sell his commission to support his wife and family.

He also sold the white spinel, and from that moment on its history is sketchy. We know that a London firm bought the gold and rubies with which it had been mounted. We know that experts tested the stone and found it to be a genuine white spinel, amazed though they were.

We know that in the middle of the nineteenth century the stone itself was offered for sale at the French Court. But the sale did not go through.

This is the last that we know of the white spinel. It has disappeared from the pages of history and is waiting somewhere—for you to find it.

There is always a chance, of course, that another white spinel might be dug out of the earth, or picked up by a rockhound. Although Ceylon has long been famous for its occurrences of spinels, there are other locations where this gem may be found. Burma and Siam grounds yield spinel, and in the United States spinels are found in Orange County, New York, and Sussex County, New Jersey.

Perhaps there is another white spinel, even here in the dirt and rocks of the United States, waiting for some lucky treasure hunter to find it. Who knows? All it takes is a little luck—and the knowledge of what you are looking for.

What makes the white spinel (or another white spinel, if you can find one) so rare is the color, or rather the lack of color. All genuine spinels, with the exception of the famous white gem, are colored. Probably the best known of these is the so-called ruby, or red, spinel. The Black Prince's Ruby in the British Crown jewels is a fine example of a red spinel.

It was after World War II that American gem makers began making their fine, synthetic spinels which can now be bought almost anywhere, but these are as nothing compared to the real article.

The real article, this white spinel of Kandy, is unique, the truly one and only, a gem so rare that most people do not even know that it ever existed.

This fantastic stone will one day be found by some treasure hunter who is aware that there is such a thing as a white spinel. But he must look for it. And, if he finds it, he can name his own price.

THERE are treasure stories about the royal gems of almost every nation in the world. The trouble, however, is that it is almost impossible to either prove or disprove these tales of royal baubles.

Sometimes it is difficult to prove or disprove the story of a find—such as the "finding" of the necklace which Napoleon gave to Josephine. This was, allegedly, a necklace of gold which through the vicissitudes of time had disappeared.

Through a long chain of circumstances, the necklace finally came into the hands of a young couple, both in love and both needing money. The husband had been out of work, and, as time went on, he became desperate for money, so desperate that he took a chance on an old piece of "junk"—a necklace he believed to be of worthless imitation gold.

He took it to a pawnshop in the hope that he could get something, even a little money, for it. The pawnbroker fingered the necklace, then excitedly examined it through an eyepiece, and exclaimed that the young man had brought him one of the finds of the century.

One version of the story has the young man receiving over $20,000 for the necklace. For what the jeweler had found on the inside of the links were the engraved initials N and J. This was the necklace that Napoleon had given to Josephine.

Yet in trying to check the story this writer can find no verification. Mr. William J. Fielding of famous Tiffany and Co., in New York, has this to say of the necklace story: "With regard to the necklace which Napoleon gave to Josephine, stories relating to this necklace pop up from time to time and upon trying to run them down, they seem apocryphal."

Certainly this should at least cast doubts upon this particular treasure "find."

SOMETIMES the problem is to find out whether a particular royal bauble is missing—and not whether or not it was ever found. Two examples of this type are the opal which belonged to the Roman senator Nonius, and the emerald table of the treasury of the ancient Goths.

The first of these, the opal, was a very lovely gem—and Marc Antony wanted it despite the fact that it was the property of Nonius. The gem was considered to be one of the largest in the ancient world, as well as one of the loveliest. The Romans themselves placed a value of $100,000 (in terms of our money) on it, and, when Marc Antony made clear that he desired the stone, Nonius preferred exile to giving it up.

Today I can find no trace of this stone. It could be in a museum; I don't know. It is physically impossible to check with every museum and historical archive in the world. Yet the Gemological Institute of

America has no knowledge of it, and neither has Cartier's Inc., of New York.

Chances are that the stone is lost. And, if it could be found, while the actual value of the stone might not be very much, at least the historical value would be fabulous—if it is actually missing.

So also with the other treasure mentioned above, the emerald table of the treasury of the ancient Goths.

According to Edward Gibbon in *The History of the Decline and Fall of the Roman Empire,* there was such a table in the treasury of the Goths—and what a fantastic work of art this must have been.

The top of the table was cut from a single piece of emerald. Surrounding the top were three rows of pearls, and the top was supported by three hundred and sixty-five feet of gems and gold. Such was the table that was in the treasury of the ancient Goths when the Arabs plundered it.

Did the Arabs take the table? I don't know for certain. Again, there is no way of checking this without checking with every museum in the world.

Yet it seems to me that, if the table of the Goths were still in existence, it would be an item that everyone would know about.

If it is missing—and if you can find it, your fortune is made.

Sometimes of course there is another kind of uncheckable story. There is a story of a "find." You can verify it—but you cannot verify the fact that the find is worth anything after it has been found, such as the alleged Braganza diamond which belonged to the King of Portugal. The gem is still in the Portuguese treasury.

We know the gem was found in the 1700's in a dry bed of a river by three criminals who had been exiled to the wilds of Brazil. After finding the diamond, they hoped that possession of it would buy them leniency—and they were right. Their crimes were pardoned.

The diamond passed into the royal treasury of Portugal, where it still rests today. Yet the mystery remains. We know that the three men found the gem. We know where it is. What we do not know is whether or not it is really a diamond.

The size of the gem is one thousand, six hundred and eighty carats, second in size only to the great Cullinan diamond prior to its cutting. If the Braganza is really a diamond, then its value is fabulous, one estimate of its worth having been given as £300,000,-000, yet there is such a mystery regarding this gem that no one really knows much about it.

The gem has raised doubts in the minds of the authorities. Most of them seem to think the gem is a white topaz, and not a diamond at all. One reason for this doubt is that the gem has never been examined by an expert. The gem has not even been shown in over a hundred years.

We have descriptions of the stone; e.g., it is of a yellow shade, round, etc., yet the description leads the experts to think it resembles a white topaz far more than it does a diamond.

The Portuguese treasury keeps the gem almost like a state secret —and with good reason if it is really only a topaz, and not a diamond.

Three men found it in a dry river bed. The Kings of Portugal owned it! Yet what was it, or, rather, what is it?

There are also the stories of royal gems which are so well known to lovers of lost treasure tales that they are accepted by everyone. Yet even with all background information available, they are still listed as missing, such as the lost rubies of a goddess, a Korean idol. This loss is the treasure hunter's gain—if he can find her missing rubies. At one time, the story goes, the rubies were a part of the jewels of the French court, but today they are believed to be somewhere in the United States.

Years ago they were stolen and placed within the body of a clay cat in a ceramic factory in Germany. The thief was shot before he could reveal the hiding place of the gems. Before it was discovered where the rubies were, the cat was shipped to America and sold.

Somewhere in the United States today there is a small, aged, clay cat carrying within its innards a fortune in royal rubies.

Watch for the cat—and for other "royal" *objets d'art* from early America, when, although we did not have royalty, we did have our own way of rewarding our great men with gifts. These gifts usually were in the form of "freedom boxes."

In those days of early America, when a famous guest came to visit a city, the city fathers conferred the "freedom of the city" upon him, much as today the key to the city is given to a visiting celebrity. In former days, however, the symbol of freedom was not a key but a parchment, but since one could not very well simply present a parchment, special boxes were made to hold it. These boxes were sometimes made of silver or gold. Sometimes they were encrusted with precious gems.

Among the men who received freedom boxes were Alexander Hamilton and the Marquis de Lafayette.

There were others who also received these boxes, and it is almost a certainty that all the boxes which were conferred upon various famous guests in different cities have not found their way into the museums of the nation.

Take another look at that old box you have in the attic. Maybe that metal is not junk, as you thought. And maybe the stones are not rhinestones. Perhaps it is really gold encrusted with diamonds. In a treasure hunt, you never know.

While these freedom boxes are not royal baubles, they do belong in the same class, for ours is not a country of royalty, and perhaps these boxes are the closest American versions to lost royal gems. At least they are worth your time and effort in searching for them, for some of them are worth a fortune.

V

PAPERWEIGHTS AND BUTTONS

Odds and Ends of Great Value

THE seller listed it as a "yellow overlay weight."

The place of the sale was London. The price the buyer paid for this "weight" was over seven thousand dollars.

This sale was made not too long ago, and to the uninformed it might seem that a weight or a scale, and probably a solid gold one, had been sold for $7,000.

Or possibly it could have been a weight of a completely different kind—but whatever the uninformed guesses, the collector knows that it was a glass paperweight.

Almost everyone in America has seen, or owned, a glass paperweight at some time or other. What they do not know is that many of these weights are worth a great deal of money.

The possessor of a rare paperweight can ask almost anything, within reason, from collectors of these glass paperweights. They are as avid in their search for rare specimens as any antique car collector, philatelist, or numismatist.

They know the rare items and they want them, and if you can find a rare and antique example which they can add to their collections they are willing to pay the price for it.

Prices for glass paperweights vary, of course, and the worth of any one particular specimen depends upon many factors. First, the weight must be a rare one. It must be one of a kind or an example of a type that is rare. A paperweight which is just exactly like thousands of other paperweights could not be of any great value. But, if you can find one that is unique, a high value for that paperweight is almost assured.

Second, condition of the paperweight is an important factor determining its value. It is obvious that a weight that is damaged or in poor condition could hardly have the same value as a similar weight in fine condition.

Third, the desire for any one particular weight on the part of the collector is another prime criterion in ascertaining value. A collector who needs a certain paperweight to round out his collection usually, more willingly, pays more for a paperweight than a collector who merely wishes for, but does not really need, a particular weight.

Prices for weights which are not too rare range from $1 to $100. Certain types of overlay glass paperweights have sold for as high as $500. Weights which are considered more unique are valued up to several thousand dollars, and certain specimens such as the yellow overlay weight mentioned above, sell for $7,000 and more.

When looking for these glass paperweights it is well to remember that there are certain particular items worth watching for and there are certain facts which the searcher should keep in mind.

Overlay glass paperweights, for example, have separate contrasting layers of colors. Other types worth watching for would be the glass paperweights made of Baccarat glass, so called because they were made in the glass works at Baccarat, France. These weights are lovely examples of the art. They are generally made of red glass and usually filled with the artificial snow that is so familiar to lovers of paperweights. Made in the middle nineteenth century, these fine weights should be on the treasure hunter's list.

There is another type of paperweight worth watching for: teardrop paperweights, the glass containing patterns of air bubbles, and the air bubbles resembling tears. These paperweights were made in Massachusetts in the latter part of the nineteenth century and, technically, they are made of Pairpoint glass. Well worth watching for.

There are also paperweights made of "glass of a thousand flowers." They are the so-called Millefiori glass paperweights, the name stemming from the type of glass they are made of. The glass resembles small flowers, because when the glass is manufactured, it is composed of many small, colored-glass rods which are heated until they blend together. After this blending, the glass is cut across, resulting in a design that is like many small colored flowers.

This, then, is the glass that was used for Millefiori paperweights, collectors' items which every treasure hunter should be on the lookout for. Remember, however, that there have been thousands of Millefiori weights made, and only the oldest and rarest are worth a great deal of money.

Although it is not a paperweight, there is yet another type of glass ball which should be on the treasure hunter's list. This is the "witch ball" which frightened and superstitious Englishmen hung in their windows during the eighteenth and nineteenth centuries, when people still believed in witches.

It was thought that these balls would keep the witches away. Whether they did or not, they were certainly important items in the homes of superstitious Englishmen, just as today they are important to the treasure hunter.

They were pretty items, being made of hollow glass, the glass lined with gay colors. The glass of which these balls were made is called Nailsea Glass, since it was produced in Nailsea, England.

Perhaps they will not keep the witches away from you, but they will bring the collectors to your door, if you happen to possess one of them.

Owning a rare and unique glass ball or paperweight will certainly attract collectors, but there are certain general facts to keep in mind when dealing with paperweights. One of these is that there are many modern weights which look like rare and antique models. Although they were made honestly for merchandising reasons, it is easy to confuse a modern weight with an old one.

Also, there are fake antique weights. Though there are not many of these fakes around, it is wise to be certain that the weight you have is authentic—and there are several ways of doing this.

One way, of course, is to ask the experts. But, possibly, it would be wise to do a certain amount of preliminary research before attempting to subject your weight to the scrutiny of an expert. Probably the best and easiest way to do this is to examine the books at your local library. Usually available are two particular books, both of them fine works on glass paperweights. One of these is *French Antique Paperweights,* by Paul Jokelson; another which I recommend is *Old Glass Paperweights,* by Mrs. Evangeline Bergstrom.

Within the pages of these two books the researcher will find approximately four hundred photographs of paperweights, both the common or garden variety and the most rare and unique. Check your own paperweight against the weights shown on the pages of these books. And maybe your luck will be good, perhaps even good enough to match the value of the yellow overlay which sold for over $7,000.

SOMEWHERE in a trunk in your attic, or in an old box in your basement, or tucked away in an old desk, might be a button which could bring you a fortune.

Old buttons become more rare with every passing day, probably because they are small and easy to lose, and many times they are simply thrown away because most people never stop to think that such a thing as a button could be worth anything.

Unfortunately for the treasure hunter, there does not seem to be any way of measuring the value of a particular button, and they are among the items which you must sell for whatever the market will bear.

The value of the button depends upon many things—condition, workmanship, and, above all, it must be rare enough for it to be badly desired as a collector's item.

There are, however, general rules in watching for button treasures. By this I mean there are certain buttons worth watching for.

Even before the dawn of recorded history, men used buttons made of bone. There have been buttons taken from the ancient tombs of the Egyptians. Excavations have brought up ancient Greek buttons. And where these have been found, there are more.

The buttons of the Middle Ages go back to the 1200's and are considered museum pieces. By the 1300's buttons were made of silver and gold, and set with gem stones—a fortune for the man who finds one in good condition. These buttons of the 1300's are hallmarked, and it is relatively simple to verify a button's authenticity for this period. Some of these buttons were also set with miniatures and ivory carvings. Any one of them is a real find for the treasure hunter.

At the time of the Renaissance fine buttons became a necessity to the well dressed. The Italian cavaliers were noted for the feathers in their caps, and to fasten these feathers they used golden but-

ILLUSTRATIONS

10 to 17

10. Beautiful example of the work of the 16th century Florentine master, Benevenuto Cellini (1500-1571). This cup of gold and enamel is called the Rospigliosi cup. (*Ch. VIII*)

43

11. This is an angel from Leonardo da Vinci's "Madonna of the Rocks." Legend has it that the model for the angel was Cecilia Gallerani, and that da Vinci made another painting of this young lady—a painting now lost. If it could be found, it would be a major event in art history. (*Ch. IX*)

12. A fine example of a ship's figurehead, a Ship "Grandee," now in a museum. There are still many such figureheads in attics, junk shops, second-hand stores, etc., waiting to be discovered. (*Ch. X*)

13. The "Chalice of Antioch," a famous example of early Christian metalwork of the 4th or 5th century. This cup was found near Antioch, Syria. It might have been the Holy Grail itself, but it is not; the Holy Grail is still missing. *(Ch. XI)*

14. Captain Cugnot's steam-powered vehicle of 1770, now in the Conservatoire National des Arts et Metiers, at Paris. A vehicle made by Cugnot one year earlier is missing. *(Ch. XII)*

Courtesy of The Smithsonian Institution

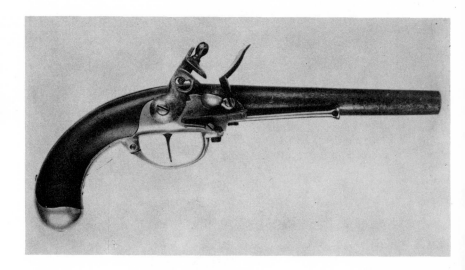

15. Two of the most eagerly sought of all American firearms are (top) the Colt Model 1847 (Whitneyville-Walker) revolver and the U. S. Model 1799 flint-lock pistol (bottom). The "Walker" was the first revolver adopted by any army and was the heaviest (4 lbs. 9 oz.). In top condition, this revolver sells for $5,000; only a hundred or so are known to exist. Some 2,000 of the flintlock pistol were made in 1799-1800 by Simeon North of Berlin, Conn., but less than a dozen are known today. In mint condition it is worth twice its weight (3 lbs. 4 oz.) in gold. Out of the 2,000 pistols made, more than twelve must surely still exist—somewhere. *(Ch. XIII)*

16. Three examples of rare miniatures. At left is the painting of Judge Thomas Waties by Charles Fraser (1782-1860). Center, a miniature of David McClellan attributed to Benjamin Trott (c.1770-c.1841). At right, a fine miniature of Otto, Count de Mosloy, by Charles W. Peale (1741-1799), the artist who painted our nation's most famous portrait of George Washington. (*Ch. XIV*)

17. This missing painting by Frederick Remington is worth $25,000—if you can find it. It is shown above as part of an advertisement. (*Ch. XV*)

Courtesy of National Distillers Products Co.

50

tons. And these cavalier buttons were made by such master craftsmen as the world may never see again.

Cellini was one of them, and if you can find a button made by this
man, who is still considered to be the finest goldsmith the world has
ever known, your fortune is made.

Cavalier buttons were also made by the Pollaiuoli, both Antonio
and his brother Pierre as well as Matteo del Pollaiuolo. Finiguerra
was another craftsman who made these golden buttons, fitting ornaments for holding the feathers on the caps of the cavaliers.

The ladies of the Renaissance were also noted for their use of buttons of fine craftsmanship. They fastened their robes with these buttons, and it is important to note that brass buttons were also used by
the ladies of this period.

There are many missing buttons of the pre-revolutionary days in
France—an era when buttons were so popular that one of the
French Kings, Francis I (1494-1547), used more than thirteen
thousand buttons on one outfit! Others of the court imitated their
rulers, and for several centuries buttons were objects of fantastic
workmanship, so much so that at one time the cost of buttons alone
became a major expenditure of the French state.

Buttons were made of precious metal and decorated with every
fine gem stone known to man. Diamonds and rubies were considered fitting for these items of extravagance. Many, many of the buttons of this period are missing, and fortune awaits the person who
can find any of them today.

American buttons are also collectors' items. Buttons made in
America—if you can find the right ones—are of value. The number
of buttons made at first was small, so small in fact that the metal
buttons on the uniforms of the American revolutionary soldiers were
made in France.

However, some buttons were made. Among the most famous of
these, of course, are those made by Caspar Wistar, who made buttons in Philadelphia as early as 1750. These buttons were metal, and
so far no marked brass buttons made by Wistar have been found.
Perhaps you might be the lucky finder.

Certain colonial buttons considered rarities are the odd-shaped
metal buttons. Any metal button from this period which is not of the
regular round shape is worth investigating.

There is a type of very rare button which is set with marcasite, a substance which looks like diamond. These buttons were very popular during the period of the 1700's, yet today an example of a marcasite-set button is considered a rarity.

Also from this period are buttons by a man whose name is familiar to every schoolboy—Paul Revere. Known as a silversmith, Revere also made buttons. And these buttons are marked, therefore easily recognizable and just waiting to be found.

There are all kinds of buttons wanted by collectors, and among these are listed the buttons made by Wedgwood: cameos set in ivory and gold, and silver.

From the 1800's date the buttons marked with the name of Williston. Though they are cloth-covered buttons, they are nevertheless collectors' items.

There are buttons marked "Hurd" which are worth watching for; also buttons made of pewter, marked "I.C.H. Lancaster"—another type worth watching for.

Charm strings of buttons—strings on which are many different kinds of buttons—are familiar items to the collectors. They, also, are very valuable. But never make the mistake of breaking the string. Take the charm string intact to an expert and let him decide upon the value of the buttons thereon, or on the value of the charm string as a whole. These charm strings, although once popular in the 1800's, are becoming rarer by the day. And as they become more rare, their value soars up, fortunately for the treasure hunter.

Even the molds in which the buttons were made are items valued by the collectors. These molds are from the 1700's mostly and can be either of metal or of wood, but by far the rarer of the two types is the wooden mold since this has not withstood the test of time as well as the metal mold.

Whatever you find, have it checked by an expert. There are buttons and buttons—and they are all worth looking for. Whether they are buttons of gold and silver, with their embellishments of diamonds and emeralds and fine gem stones, or whether they are brass buttons of the Renaissance or the golden cavalier buttons by Cellini —they mean a fortune for you if you can find them.

VI

SILVER ON THE C SCALE

Musical Instruments and Lost Scores

EVERY treasure hunter in the world knows the story of the "Strads," the missing Stradivarius violins which mean a fortune to anyone who can find one.

Yet, the finding of a "Strad" is an amusing paradox even to the veteran treasure hunter: since everyone knows about them, there obviously are no "Strads" left—or someone would have found them by now.

The skeptics claim that if anyone, anyone at all, had a "Strad" he would be aware of it because the information is so widely known.

One fact, however, which the skeptics have overlooked completely is that Antonio Stradivari (1644-1737) made approximately eleven hundred violins—yet only about six hundred of them have ever been found!

Simple subtraction shows that there are approximately five hundred Stradivarius violins which have never been found—and five hundred violins simply do not disappear from the face of the earth. Some may have been destroyed, a few may have been damaged beyond repair, but somewhere there are enough "Strads" to make a fortune for anyone who can find them.

The price you could get for a Stradivarius would depend, of course, upon the condition of the instrument. In fine condition it could demand a very high price. I have seen prices for a "Strad" range from $13,000 to $80,000.

One other factor that would determine the value of a "Strad" would be the incontrovertible authenticity of the instrument. Naturally, over the years there have been many fakes produced—naturally, because a fake, if it could be palmed off as the genuine article, would bring the maker a great deal of money.

There are, however, various ways by which the experts can tell whether or not a certain instrument is authentic or not.

One method of helping to identify a "Strad" is by comparing the instrument with Stradivari sketches, some of which are in the local museum at Cremona, Italy. Also, the science of acoustics is a great deal of help in identifying authentic "Strads." An acoustical laboratory is being set up in Cremona by the *Scuola Internazionale di Liuteria* for this purpose.

Experts can check the tone of a violin. They can check the "varnish." There are many ways of telling whether or not what you have is actually a "Strad," but before you take your violin to the experts there is one way you yourself can tell whether or not it is at least called a Stradivarius. This is by looking on the *inside* of the instrument.

If you are lucky there will be on the *inside* part of the violin a label, proclaiming it to have been made by Stradivari. Yet here again you must watch for the fake, for it was here that the violin forger marked his model—the label just as much a fake as the violin he had just manufactured.

If you do have a Stradivarius you will have something very rare in the world of music. Before the time of Stradivari (and Nicolò Amati, who taught him) the violin was not the instrument we know today. It had a shrill sound, and it was only the work of these masters that gave their violins the sweet tone which, even today, is considered to be the very finest of violin tones in the world. It has never been excelled.

The shape and size of each piece of a violin are measured to a hair's-breadth in the making, and Stradivari was the master at it. Thus his violins have the magnificent tones that have fascinated music lovers since the 1700's—tones which today can bring you a fortune if you can find a violin that can produce them.

But the "Strad" is not the only violin which the treasure hunter should watch for. It would be rather horrible if, in his search for a "Strad," the treasure hunter should pass by a Guarnerius, because these violins made by Guarnieri are worth many thousands of dollars.

Most authorities rank the Guarnerius violin second to the Stradivarius, although there are many who consider the Guarnerius to be equal to if not better than the "Strad" itself.

Guarnieri was an Italian, born 1683, died 1745. His full name was Giuseppe Antonio Guarnieri del Gesù. The del Gesù part of his name, however, was added as a result of the nickname "del Gesù" which was given to him because he inscribed I.H.S. on his labels—an important fact for the treasure hunter to remember.

There were other members of this family who also made violins, but it is del Gesù whose violins are the most famous and the most valuable and, as a result, the most desired by the treasure hunter.

The Guarnerius violin, the Stradivarius violin, and one other instrument—the Bergonzi cello!

Bergonzi was a pupil of Stradivari and from him learned to make magical instruments that even today are famous both for their extraordinarily beautiful tones and their beautiful shapes.

Every music lover and every owner of a music store wait for the day when they will find a Bergonzi. Such was the case of Jan Paul, owner of a music store in San Francisco, when he purchased six second-hand musical instruments. They had belonged to a musician who was moving and who had to dispose of the instruments.

Paul took all six off his hands for the nominal sum of $2,600. However, when Paul finally had them in his own store, he noticed that one of the cellos seemed different from the rest.

A violin-maker in his own right, Jan Paul examined the instrument carefully. He cleaned it with caution, not really knowing what he might find—but always hoping to find, as every lover of fine instruments does, a rare instrument.

Once the cello was cleaned, Paul realized he had made his find. The instrument was made in 1733 by Carlo Bergonzi of Italy. Over two hundred years old, the instrument was valued at $6,500.

Today there are other Bergonzi cellos missing—each waiting for the treasure hunter to recognize it as one of the most beautiful musical instruments ever made.

WHEN Francis Scott Key first had the inspiration for writing the *Star Spangled Banner* as he watched the attack on Fort McHenry, he had no paper with him and he scribbled the now immortal song on the back of an old letter.

Unfortunately, for the treasure hunter, this letter is now the property of the Walters Art Gallery, and the flag which Key described as "the Star Spangled Banner" is now in the National Museum in Washington, D.C.

However, even if these objects are safely in the hands of the museums, there are "first" copies of the *Star Spangled Banner* which are missing, and which could bring over $3,000 to the treasure hunter if he can find a copy.

The Carr first sheet music edition of the *Banner* should be on your treasure list. These editions have sold for anywhere from $1,000 to over $3,000 each.

At the Parke-Bernet Galleries, New York, a very rare first edition of the *Banner* was recently sold for over $3,000.

Although the actual price paid for this copy is undisclosed, it is known that it was well over $3,000 since there were two other bidders who had quoted above this price, and they had underbid the actual buyer.

Not even the Library of Congress has a first edition of the *Banner*, but maybe you do—in that old trunk in your attic, in the storage bin in the basement, or hidden between the pages of your old family bible.

Prices quoted for the *Banner* are known prices paid for copies which have been held up for auction, but there is much discrepancy in the field of music as to listed prices for rare treasures and the actual prices which the collectors will pay.

In order to sell rare music, you must have an authentic copy first —and then find a collector who wants it badly. Some collectors, for example, would pay almost any price for a collection of Caruso's records on the old Victor label. Others would not give you a dime for them. Jazz lovers are always in the market for the early jazz records, but lovers of classical music would not think they were even worth bidding for.

A point in illustration would be the scores of Victor Herbert, with particular reference to Herbert's operetta, *Prince Ananias*. A copy of *Prince Ananias* could turn up at any time almost anywhere and be sold for as little as $5, yet there is one collector who has gathered together the scores of all of Herbert's operettas—with the exception of the score for *Prince Ananias*. He has made an offer of $100 to anyone who can sell him a copy of it, an offer of two thousand percent over what the score would sell for normally.

It is, therefore, important to find a collector who really wants what you have found. The treasure hunter can only say "It was missing and I have found it. What will you pay for it?"

This, however, would be a simple question for anyone who could find the missing music from *Thespis*, the musical debut of Gilbert and Sullivan, this famous duo of the English operatic stage.

All of the music of *Thespis* has disappeared with the exception of one song, "Little Maid of Arcadee," and one chorus, "Climbing Over Rocky Mountain."

"Little Maid of Arcadee" has not disappeared, because it was published as a separate ballad. "Climbing Over Rocky Mountain" has not disappeared, because it was used again in *The Pirates of Penzance*.

Today, certain collectors badly want the missing parts of the score of *Thespis*. Many people have tried to find this music—and they have failed. Yet perhaps you will be luckier than they and return the missing music from *Thespis* to a world of music lovers who will reach out eagerly for it.

This music of Gilbert and Sullivan would, of course, be valuable, because it is the work of such famous composers, but sometimes missing music is important because it is indicative of a certain period or age from which few examples are extant.

For example, the period of Colonial (pre-Revolutionary) America. During this era many songs were written, yet material from that time is almost negligible in either printed or manuscript form.

Any printed score or musical manuscript from this period would be worth investigation. At least there is one surviving relic of Colonial music. This is a priceless manuscript, dated 1759, which contains four songs by Francis Hopkinson (1737-1791). This manuscript is now in the Library of Congress.

There are, of course, many missing manuscripts, and here, again, as with so much in the music field, the only thing you can say is that they are missing. And if you can find them they will be worth whatever the collectors are willing to pay, and if you are lucky the collectors will be willing to pay a great deal.

A contemporary of Hopkinson's was James Lyon, who was also a composer, and yet, unlike Hopkinson, none of his songs are extant today—unless one might be found in your attic or in that perennial old trunk in the basement.

Another musician from the same period whose works are also missing is William Billings, who wrote secular music.

Another gentleman of roughly the same period (1767-1836) is, however, a musician of some mystery, and we have no idea of whether or not you should look for his music. Not only because there is no way of telling how much the collectors would pay for his missing music, but because we do not know whether or not he ever even wrote music.

Was he a songwriter or wasn't he, is a question which very much bothers the historians of early American music. There is a great deal of doubt as to whether or not this man, by name Johann Christian Gottlieb Graupner, actually composed any music at all. It is a supposition that he did. It is at least known to be a fact that he was one of the leading musicians of the city of Boston, and it seems more than likely that he did compose, but, if he did, his songs have never been found.

Perhaps you will be the one to find a missing song by Graupner—and fill in one of the missing pages of our nation's musical history—and if the collectors want the manuscript badly enough, fill your pocketbook as well.

VII

AFTER THE BATTLE

The Loot of Many Wars

SOMETIMES when the chaos of war is over, loot, fabulous in value, fantastic in historic worth, is scattered all over the globe. Sometimes it is distributed as booty to the soldiers who have done their job well. Other times it is disposed of with the help and advice of the authorities. And sometimes it is lost—never to be found again.

Where are these "casualties" of battle? Many of them have been destroyed in the many and varied wars which have raged across the face of the earth. Some of them have been burned in fires set by the soldiery, and some of them have found their way into the knapsacks and saddle bags of the soldiers.

Many times a soldier brought home a "souvenir," something he thought might make a pretty gift for the girl back home. What he actually brought back is a magnificent treasure from the castles and homes of a looted and defeated nation.

Often the loot was distributed as booty by the commanders, as was the case with the rug of Khosrau, which was not just any rug, but a creation made for the audience hall of the Persian king, Khosrau, who ruled in the sixth century.

The rug was designed to represent a common enough motif, that of eternal spring, yet the design was so fabulous that it has never been forgotten.

Barley fields of emeralds formed the border. Paths in the rug's landscape were paths of pearls, and the brooks were made of stones which probably were diamonds. Even common dirt became gold in this magnificent specimen of the rug maker's art.

Cost of this fantastic rug? $200,000,000. The rug was designed for the audience hall of a king, yet the king was not to retain his rug, for the Byzantines attacked and Khosrau fled before them.

His rug was the price he paid for his retreat. His captors took his fabulous rug, fit only for a king, and cut it up and distributed it as war booty—one fifth to Caliph Omar; another large piece to Ali; and the rest was cut up and handed over, piece by piece, to sixty thousand soldiers who, in their turn, sold their pieces. Perhaps, if you are lucky enough, you might find one of the small but still fabulous pieces of the rug of Khosrau.

Sometimes loot is disposed of with the help and advice of the authorities. There was an eighteenth-century jade altar set which was disposed of in this way.

Lord James Bruce Elgin, English soldier, commanded the troops at Peking, China, in the year 1860. At this time the Summer Palace was looted and burned. The booty taken during this burning included the jade altar set, which was then sold under the direct supervision of the military.

The set was purchased by a British officer in Peking and remained in the hands of his family until 1949, when Gump's, in San Francisco, acquired the set, which they evaluated at $22,000.

Sometimes there is a general type of *objet d'art* missing. Because there are so many of that type extant—yet no particular one is definitely known to be missing—the best course to follow is to simply keep your eyes open, knowing that someday, sooner or later, you will run across a supreme example of that particular type of *objet d'art*.

There were, in the past, carvings of ivory made that were so fine that they upheld the highest standards of art experts. Yet, though there were many such pieces produced, mostly in the thirteenth, fourteenth and fifteenth centuries, war swept across the lands and the ivories became lost.

In England, during the Reformation, many of these carvings were lost, as well as in France during the Revolution. Marvelous examples of this art were perhaps lost forever unless the treasure hunter can locate them and place them in the hands of the collectors or the museum curators, where they belong.

There were some pieces saved, of course, like the thirteenth-century casket which is today in the Kensington Museum; but there is still an uncounted number of missing ivories, displaced by reform and revolution, hiding perhaps in some country town in Europe or in the backwaters of America where someone took them without even knowing what they were. They are waiting for someone to recognize them for the treasures they are.

Often, after the battle is over, one does not even know what is missing or what to look for.

America was at war with England, and in August of 1814, two years after the start of the War of 1812, British troops entered the city of Washington. The sun had gone down, and darkness shrouded the city as the British troops invaded, accomplishing their purpose almost without resistance.

They gutted almost every official building in the city with fire, including the Capitol, the Treasury, and the bridge over the Potomac. Some of the smaller private residences also went to the torch. The only official public building which they did not set afire was the one which was the combination Post Office and Patent Office.

The most important of all the buildings they burned, from the standpoint of tradition, was the White House, and with it they destroyed items which would be of great importance to the students of Early Americana—if they could find them.

What objects may have been saved from the fire in the White House, by loyal Americans, or even, perhaps, by British troops, no one knows. It is not known what pieces of furniture, state papers, books or paintings were burnt, and since descriptions of the furnishings of the White House up to the time of the burning are inadequate, we may never know what was saved and what was destroyed by the fire.

That is why there is no way of telling what the treasure hunter should look for in his search for treasures from the White House as it was before the fire.

If you own or find something which can be proven, by papers or family traditions (verifiable of course), to have been in the White House at the time of the burning, having been removed shortly before or during that great holocaust, then surely you have a piece of Americana which would be well worth having appraised by an expert.

There is only one of the items about which we have definite knowledge. This is the large painting of George Washington which was then hanging in the White House. As every school child knows, it was Dolly Madison who saved this painting, but we have no information about any of the other items which were there at that time.

Maybe they were destroyed in the fire, and maybe one of them is in your attic, saved perhaps by an ancestor or possibly bought in a second-hand store after having been bought and sold generation after generation by people who did not know what they had. Perhaps, when you find it, you will know what it is and where it came from—and head with it for the nearest museum.

SOMETIMES, information on war loot is harder to find than the actual war loot itself, as, for example, the "lost treasures" of the Civil War. Though not strictly "loot," they are a case in point.

There are numerous stories about the treasures buried by the southerners—in the walls of their plantations and in the spacious grounds of their homes—when the Yankees invaded. But no matter where you look, the treasures seem to have evaporated as though they were genies of the air.

From such sources as the Library of Congress, the Chambers of Commerce in Harrisonburg, Virginia, Savannah, Georgia, and Richmond, Virginia, and from Cliff Arquette of Gettysburg, comes a dearth of information—because there is no information to be had.

Often other cities are suggested; sometimes it is pointed out that much of the "lost treasure" was restored after the war; sometimes the files do not disclose any treasures at all, and sometimes the files are so extensive that it is impossible to search through them.

The cities of the north which were invaded by the Rebels have also been suggested as possible places to search for buried war treasure, but here, again, the stories are nebulous.

No one seems to know exactly where the treasures might be, and this, certainly, is not due to any lack of effort on the part of treasure hunters. It may be because there really is a lack of Civil War treasure.

There might be something left, however, buried in an old garden, hidden in an old trunk, or buried behind the wallpaper and bricks of another day. If there is—and you find it—you have hit a bonanza in a very barren field.

But don't give up. Wherever there has been a skirmish, a battle, or a full-scale war, there is good hunting ground for the treasure seeker. When armies invade, people hide their valuables—and occasionally they don't live long enough to claim their property, leaving it for future generations to find.

AN American soldier was two thousand feet into the innards of the earth in a salt mine near the town of Bernterode, Austria. His job was to remove dynamite from the mine which only shortly before had belonged to the Germans.

Yet there was something in the mine besides dynamite, something he did not expect to find: a concrete wall! After some discussion with his officer, it was decided that if it was important enough for the Germans to build a concrete wall to protect something, it was important enough for the Americans to dig it out.

After arduously breaking a small hole through the six-foot thick concrete, the soldier crawled through, and the first thing he saw was a painting of a nude woman. Outside the wall his commanding officer was utterly amazed when he heard the excited shouts of the soldier: "Here's a nude! My God, it must be art!"

It was art. What the soldier had seen was only one of the paintings of the great French collection from Potsdam, Germany. Yet not only were these famous paintings hidden here by the Germans but there were also the coffin of Frederick the Great, the coffins of Marshal Paul von Hindenburg and his wife, swords that had belonged to Frederick the Great, and the crown jewels of the Hohenzollerns.

Finding these lost treasures was a part of America's job following World War II—helping to locate, to reassemble, and to redistribute the works of art looted by the Germans.

There were many men who helped in this great task, and there were at least two, during the course of the war, who lost their lives to the cause of preserving these works of art for future generations.

General Eisenhower himself inspected some of these works of art which had been hidden by the Germans. At Merkers, Germany, he inspected one cache which had been captured by the Third Army.

This treasure, left behind in a salt mine by the Germans during a hurried retreat, consisted of millions of dollars worth of art, bullion, and paper money.

When the Italians wanted to return the eight-ton, horse-back-mounted statue of Cosimo I de Medici to its former location, they were stymied. The Germans themselves had been unable to move the statue because it was too heavy for them, and the Italians were having almost as much trouble.

They had separated the horse from the statue of Cosimo, and they had planned to move the statue slowly, carefully and majestically in two parts, a job that might have taken weeks. The Yanks appraised the situation and casually loaded the statue on a tank-transport and began to move. Italians stood by the roadside shouting bravo—until it was discovered that there was another obstacle in the way. Overhead wires would obstruct the truck load.

When the bravos of the Italians faded away to groans, an American GI climbed up into the truck bed and from there he vaulted, à la Wyatt Earp or one of the James brothers, onto the saddle of Cosimo's horse. The truck moved forward, the GI stayed in the saddle—and cut down the wires as the truck moved forward. All this to the sounds of the once again cheering Italians.

Result? One statue and one horse returned to its rightful owners. The list of these items which the Americans returned after the war is almost endless. In 1946, by count, there were more than four hundred mines, public buildings, etc., which held missing works of art, put there either for "safe-keeping" or as a part of the German loot of war.

Many of these works of art have, today, been reassembled. The Americans found one whole mountain which was filled with over one hundred thousand assorted *objets d'art*.

There are, however, to this day treasures that have never been found. Any of them which could be found today, possibly among the souvenirs a soldier brought back with him from Europe, could be worth a fortune.

Various art collections became so scattered during World War II that parts of them have never been found. In Europe, thirty-seven paintings from the Finally collection, eight from the Contini collection, as well as seven paintings from Poppi and Soci were lost.

Also still missing is one of the finest antiquities in the world. Dating from the tenth century, it is a manuscript known as the Codex Aesinas of Tacitus.

Owner of the manuscript at the time of its disappearance was Count Baldeschi Balleani of Jesi, and during the ferocity of the war the manuscript was, allegedly, safe at the Vatican. This last information is based on a statement by the overseer of the Villa Fonte d'Amo. Upon further questioning, the overseer said that the manuscript might not be at the Vatican but might be "elsewhere." However, it was his honest belief that the manuscript was safe.

The Vatican, however, stated that the manuscript was not in their hands—neither in their library nor in the *Archivio Segreto*.

To this day, the Codex has never been located.

Nor have many items from the fabled city of Florence been found, where many art treasures completely disappeared from its museums and galleries.

After the Americans took Florence they began the immense job of returning its art works and helping to repair the traditional beauty of the city. They also aided in cataloging the items they could not find, the treasures that had mysteriously disappeared during the battle.

Perhaps they were hidden so well by the Germans that they still remain hidden—and will remain hidden until some lucky finder unearths them. Perhaps they were destroyed in the course of the battle. Or maybe they were picked up, by GI souvenir hunters.

Perhaps a GI in your hometown brought home one of the items on the following list—a list compiled for me by T. Rossi, *Il Soprintendente, Soprintendenza alle Gallerie,* Florence. These items all disappeared from Florence. They are still missing.

Included in the list (sizes are given in centimeters) are the names of the galleries, etc., from which each object disappeared, the name of the artist, and its description:

GALLERIE DEGLI UFFIZI
>   (1)—Inv. 1890 #1123—Memling's School—Portrait of an unknown man. Painted on board; 0.35 x 0.24
>   (2)—Inv. 1890, #1554—Agnolo Bronzino—Christ laid down. Painted on copper; 0.42 x 0.30
>   *(3)—Inv. 1890, #8268—A. del Pollaiuolo—Hercules striking the Hydra. Painted on board; 0.175 x 0.112
>   *(4)—Inv. 1890 #1478—A. del Pollaiuolo—Hercules killing Antaeus. Painted on board; 0.16 x 0.95

* (*Since the first printing of this book, the two paintings, items 3 and 4 on the list, have been found in California.*)

(5)—Inv. 1890 #2185—Lorenzo di Credi—Self portrait. Painted on board; 0.34 x 0.30

NATIONAL MUSEUM

(1) Sculpture Inv. No. 59—Pierino da Vinci—Virgin nursing her child, and Saints. Marble relief

(2) Sculpture Inv. No. 94—Italian art of the end of XVI Cent.— (Sometimes attributed to Michelangelo)—Faun's mask

PALATINA GALLERY (Pitti Palace)

(1) Inv. Palatina Gall. #26—Domenico Feti—The parable of the vineyard. Painted on board; 0.75 x 0.44

(2) Inv. Palatina Gall. #462—John Van Huysum—Flower vase. Painted on canvas; 0.47 x 0.35

(3) Inv. Palatina Gall. #253—In the fashion of Correggio—The Manger. Painted on board; 0.341 x 0.245

(4) Inv. Palatina Gall. #263—Bronzino's school—Christ on the Cross. Painted on board; 0.28 x 0.181

(5) Inv. Palatina Gall. #282—Van Dyck School—Virgin with the Child, and Saints. Painted on copper; 0.218 x 164.

(6) Inv. 1890 #4996—School of Bologna—Annunciation. Painted on copper; 0.35 x 0.27

UFFIZI GALLERY (ROOM OF DRAWINGS AND PRINTS)

(1) Inv. of Drawings #6127—Callot—Saint Anthony's Temptation. Pen drawings; 0.47 x 0.75

(2) Inv. of Drawings #738—Tintoretto—The body of Christ dead. Pen drawing; 0.28 x 0.69

(3) Inv. of Drawings #1774—Raffaello—The Virgin, named "of the veil." Drawing with black pencil and chalk; 0.77 x 0.73

(4) Inv. of Drawings #96774—Annibale Caracci—Figure of beardless man in the act of pulling ropes. Drawing of fragmentary carbon, cut out and applied to cardboard; 1.79 x 0.85

Where are these or any of the other treasures that were lost in the war? They just might be in the hands of GI souvenir hunters, and, if they are, they are very lucky—if they are aware of the fact.

War loot has been brought home by Yankee soldiers before. Why not this time? Possibly they brought back a work of art they enjoyed, not even beginning to realize its value or the fact that it is a masterpiece or an ancient manuscript. It may be lost forever if they do not realize what it is they have. But if they do, it could be worth a fortune.

VIII

THE TERRIBLE MAN AND THE GENIUS

The Works of Cellini and Michelangelo

WHEN, several years ago, a salt cellar made by Benvenuto Cellini was shown on an American television program, it was regarded as so valuable that even while it was in front of the cameras, in the direct view of millions of people, it was still guarded with armed men on either side of it.

A treasure beyond the reach of most, this salt cellar is so valuable because Benvenuto Cellini was the greatest goldsmith of all time, unsurpassed in the miracles he wrought with gold, silver and other precious metals.

Yet craftsmanship is a thing apart from character, and even in his own time, while recognizing his artistry as a goldsmith and sculptor, people still called him "The Terrible Man."

It was certainly descriptive of his character, for this was the man who, although a dashing enough figure, was a brawler, a swordsman and a killer. He was the Casanova of his day—leaving behind him at least three legitimate children and an untold number of illegitimate children.

Born in 1500 in Florence, Italy, he died in that same city in 1571, although in the interim he had done work in other Italian cities as well as in Florence. He worked for Francis I, Pope Clement VII, and Cosimo de Medici.

He was the confidant of kings and popes but, because of his brawling nature, he was not always in their good graces.

Argumentative, proud, easily insulted, "The Terrible Man" lived up to his name, but this did not detract from the magnificence of his works—works which, if all of them could be found, would carry a price so high that no one man could pay it.

Yet, if you could find only one of the objects he made, your fortune would be assured.

Much of his smaller works have disappeared. He was primarily a goldsmith, and naturally the objects made by a goldsmith are necessarily small. There were salt cellars and jewel boxes, buttons and jugs. All sorts of small things—and most of them lost.

There is a jug which Cellini had started but never completed, and he mentions this little jug in his autobiography. He reports it as having been stolen, along with "a great quantity of other valuable articles." He found it necessary, according to his own words, to recommence the jug, starting all over again. Thus there is, somewhere, an unfinished Cellini jug just waiting for you to find it.

This is only one of the many Cellini works known to be lost. Some of them, perhaps, were shipped to the New World in the early days of the Spanish conquistadores when they brought art from all over Europe to decorate their churches in what was then the savage wilderness.

The smaller works of Cellini's goldsmithing art could be anywhere—even in your attic. There are two reasons why these treasures must be found: first, to put them back in the museums, where they belong, and, second, to put a fortune in your pocket.

But there are other items of Cellini's which are also lost—objects he made not as a goldsmith, for, like so many artists of his day, he did not work in only one field.

He was also a sculptor. But for many years it was believed that he had never worked in marble. Yet, less than a quarter of a century ago, two marble statues, one of Apollo and one of Narcissus, were found in a garden in Florence, Italy. And they were made by Cellini. These were completely unexpected finds, because even the experts were certain that Cellini had never used marble.

Not too long ago the M. H. de Young Memorial Museum in San Francisco was given another Cellini marble—a bust representation of Cosimo de Medici, one of Cellini's patrons. Value of this latest Cellini marble? One estimate stands at a possible $500,000.

When one-time flashlight salesman Roscoe F. Oakes presented the marble to the De Young Museum, he gave them more than just $500,000 worth of Cellini art. He gave them an historic link between the art world of today and the brawling, exciting era of the sixteenth century's most "Terrible Man."

What other statues are missing, no one really knows. As I stated above, it was not even known that he had worked in marble until some of his missing statues were found.

There is, however, one series in connection with Cellini's work as a sculptor which is missing, and yet it is one which most people would never consider as being worth anything at all: the clay models which he made for a fountain at Fontainebleau and which have never been found.

Even these models of clay would be of some value if they could be found, although they would certainly not have the worth of a statue or a small piece of goldsmithing. Anything of Cellini's which you might find would have some value, and most of his works would be worth a fortune.

There are numerous treasure stories connected with the name of Cellini, as with so many fabulous men and works of the past.

There is, for example, the story of the man who was browsing through a San Francisco second-hand store. He found, the story goes, a Cellini cup, for which he paid $2. Today, that cup, still according to the story, is worth $1,000,000.

The trouble with stories of this kind is that they cannot be verified. I have heard the story many times but cannot find any basis for it. It may be true, of course, but Richard B. Gump of the famous Gump's store in San Francisco has no information on it. A verification in my own mind that the story is therefore rumor, for surely Richard Gump would at least have heard of the incident if it were authentic.

Yet even if this story is rumor, perhaps the next time you step into a second-hand store, your own find will not be rumor but could become another true anecdote in the history of treasure hunting. For to find a Cellini cup, salt cellar, jewel box or marble statue is to find a fortune.

THERE was a man who was a painter, architect and sculptor, and so great was his genius that when a thousand years have passed the world will still remember and honor his name: Michelangelo!

So intense was he, so determined that each thing he made should have perfection, and so talented, that he reached a pinnacle of artistic genius never before or since reached by man; yet even then he was never completely satisfied with his own work.

So intent was he upon portraying exactly the anatomy of the human figure that he cut up and dissected human corpses to better understand the lines and shadings he would carve into a block of inanimate stone or paint on a canvas.

There was no task Michelangelo Buonarroti would not undertake—tasks at which other artists had failed. Michelangelo accepted their challenges—and brought forth genius.

Once a huge piece of marble was brought to him, and even the great Michelangelo faltered at the thought of producing anything from it, because the marble was chipped and damaged beyond recognition. Another sculptor had attempted to make a statue from this marble but had failed miserably.

Michelangelo, however, accepted the challenge, and brought forth one of his greatest creations—a colossal David so heavy that it took forty men to move it out of his workshop when it was finished.

The David stood for over three hundred years in the central square in Florence. Today it has been moved and is now safe in the Academy in Florence.

But there was another David made by Michelangelo which, unfortunately, is not safe either in the Academy in Florence or anywhere else, as far as it is known. For this is one of the missing treasures of Michelangelo—a work which can never be matched again by any living artist.

This second David is of bronze. Shorter than the marble David in Florence, which stands eighteen feet high, this David is lifesize. It was made on order for Pierre de Rohan and was forwarded to France in 1508. It has disappeared and has been lost for over three centuries.

Three hundred years, of course, is a very long time for a work of art such as this to be on the missing list, but there is a good chance that it may yet be found. Sometimes, however, there is a better chance of finding something which has not been lost for such a long period—such as Michelangelo's statue of Hercules which disappeared in the early part of the 1700's.

Michelangelo was only seventeen when he created this statue of Hercules, which, at one time, was in the possession of the King of France. But even at seventeen Michelangelo was a genius, a genius not only in sculpture but in almost every other field of art as well.

Everyone knows of Michelangelo's great paintings, especially those in the Sistine Chapel, but his portable paintings are another story entirely. The only definitely authentic Michelangelo portable painting which is extant today hangs in the Uffizi Gallery. It is a magnificent representation of the Child, the Madonna, and Saint Joseph.

The rest are missing, lost to us forever unless the treasure hunter looks for and finds them.

There is no set value you can place on a piece of sculpture or a painting by Michelangelo, for they are numbered among the museum pieces that are considered "priceless." There are museums which would pay any price for one of his works of art.

Even his working architectural models would have value if you could find them, for, of all the clay and wooden models he made, only one example has, as far as we know, survived. This is the model for the cupola of Saint Peter's. All the rest of them are missing.

These models, of course, would not have the fantastic value of his sculpture and paintings, but they would be worth something. And they could be anywhere.

The world's great missing works of art could be anywhere at all, and anywhere is a big word. It takes in many countries and many places. All of Europe; all of America; part of Asia. Every junk pile; every attic; every second-hand store.

Like the Pennsylvania mountain second-hand store where it would have been thought impossible to find a great work of art. Yet it was here that the bust of a young girl was found. And when the experts finally got a look at it, they saw in the lines of the head the master craftsmanship of the great French artist, Auguste Rodin.

The experts were not certain, of course. The authenticity of the bust is still being investigated, but if it is by Rodin it is one of the great treasures of the world returned to us.

So with the works of Michelangelo. They could be anywhere. Even in an out-of-the-way second-hand store. The works of art which are lost are numbered in the thousands, but of all of them probably the greatest are those of Michelangelo. These treasures are waiting for you to make your fortune—if you can find them.

IX

THE MASTER'S TOUCH

Paintings by the Masters

THE room is hushed and quiet. There is only the heavy breathing of the men who are bending over an object which takes all their attention. The smell of chemicals fills the air—turpentine and alcohol; sulphuric acid; cedar oil and oil of spice. Small instruments lie ready to puncture tiny spots on the object, which is still untouched by the silent, eager men.

Suddenly the door opens and attendants wheel in an X-ray machine. The men are ready to begin. Their work is quiet; yet there is an urgency in the air, an urgency caused by the knowledge that the slightest miscalculation on their part may do irreparable damage. Their movements are calculatingly slow—because any spilling of their chemicals or slip of their instruments may cause untold damage.

The X-ray apparatus is brought forward and focused on the object they have been studying so carefully. Finally, then, they know what they have before them—and what they must do. They know that for months they will be in this room working with chemicals and instruments, and, using all their talents, they will scrape and clean and bring to life the object which they have so anxiously studied.

For what they have before them is a painting, but not just any painting. It is a very bad, poorly painted portrait. Yet by the use of chemicals and X rays they know that underneath this badly done work is another painting, a fantastic find in the world of art. A painting by one of the old masters, its marvellous colors and fabulous brush work hidden by the workings of an inferior artist who had placed his own splotchy work on top of one of the world's masterpieces because he had been too poor to buy canvas.

This is what has probably happened to many of the masterpieces of yesteryear. Where are they now? Perhaps in your attic is an old painting worthless in itself, yet beneath the top layer of paint is another painting, a painting so valuable that it could pay for your next yacht or two—if you only knew it.

So take a good, a really good, look at that old painting of yours. Perhaps you really have something.

Sometimes you can tell at a glance that one painting is underneath another one, because the top layer of paint has been damaged in some way and the older painting shows through. Most of the time, however, it takes an expert to tell, and it takes an expert to clean away the top layer of paint. Never, never try to remove it yourself. This could cause irreparable damage to the bottom painting, and irreparable damage to the value of the finer of the two paintings, a point of great importance to the treasure hunter.

There are some people who will insist upon trying a do-it-yourself method, by applying the more common paint removers such as alcohol, soap with potash, alkali or acetic acid, but remember that all of these regular paint removers remove paint at such a speed that the painting itself can become damaged. Only the experts can use the proper chemicals at the proper speed.

Only the experts can really do anything with these double paintings. They know when and how to use the proper instruments, chemicals and X-ray machine. They know all the modern ways of determining the authenticity as well as the number of layers of paint on a canvas.

X rays pass through the atom structure of the painting, and the less atoms present the easier it is for X rays to pass directly through. If there is one painting directly over another, it is harder for the X rays to penetrate both than if there were only one painting present. Thus the X ray finds the existence of the second, underneath painting.

Also, by seeing which parts of the painting the rays can penetrate most easily, the experts are able to tell quite easily whether a whole painting has been painted over or only a part of the original painting has been retouched. The latter is frequently found to be the case, since it was often simpler merely to change an older painting and bring it up to date than to paint an entirely new one.

The more prevalent custom, however, was for the artist to paint over the entire painting, leaving his own, usually hopeless, endeavor on top of what would be an enduring work of art to be hung proudly in museum halls—if it could be found.

How many paintings were lost in this way no one really knows. But there is at least one painting which may fall into this category. This is the portrait of Cesare Borgia by Pier di Lorenzo.

This painting has completely disappeared; yet, if it could be found, it would be a museum piece. Over four hundred and fifty years old, the painting may very well have been painted over. It certainly disappeared during a period when artists were notoriously poor and hungry, and any canvas within reach became the background for their art.

The portrait of the Borgia had already disappeared in the sixteenth century, in the days when canvas was still rare and expensive, so the probability is that somewhere the painting is well hidden beneath a layer of more modern art.

The portrait, of course, might not have been painted over at all but might still be in its original state. It could be that the eyes of a Borgia still stare out at a make-believe Renaissance world from the dark corner of someone's attic.

If your attic does contain this painting, it contains not just a painting by a master but the portrait of a man who made history; a man of the Renaissance who, among other things, has been accused of killing his own brother, although historians disagree on this point.

Soldier and Cardinal of the Roman Catholic Church, this then is the man that Pier di Lorenzo painted. Perhaps, if you are lucky enough, this painting is in your attic, in your basement, or in the neighborhood second-hand store, either unrecognized in its original state or painted over by a mediocre artist too poor to buy a new canvas. If so, it is just waiting for you to take it to the experts, who, with their chemicals, their instruments, and their X-ray machines, can clean and repair it.

Such was the case in the little church of Lucignano d'Arbia near Siena when the priest decided that the rather mediocre and very dirty painting above the altar needed repairing.

It was a very old, mediocre painting, but the desire for neatness if not religious compunction decided the priest to have it restored. When the workmen began on the painting, however, flakes of paint came off to reveal an eye beneath the outer layer of paint. With dispatch the painting was forwarded to Rome's Restoration Institute, where it was properly restored and cleaned over a period of many months.

When they were finished, they had uncovered the lost Madonna and Child by Simone Martini, Italian painter of the later 1200's and early 1300's. This was one of the greatest finds in art history.

Perhaps then, if you are lucky enough, that old painting you have may be the Borgia by di Lorenzo, and it will become another milestone in the history of paintings once lost, but now found and replaced by the treasure hunters of the world.

IN the world of painting is one name which is familiar to many: Cuyp, the very famous family of Dutch painters who lived and worked in the 1500's and 1600's. Their works are listed among the great masterpieces of all time.

Yet, as with many of the great masters, there was at least one of their paintings which had disappeared—a painting of the embarkation of the Pilgrims for America. It is thought that this painting was an artistic representation of the actual scene itself, so that for all time the faces of the Pilgrim Fathers would be captured for posterity.

For many years this painting had been lost, until one day it was relocated by another painter who, strangely enough, was George H. Boughton, the man who himself painted such scenes as "The Puritans Going To Church" and "The Return Of The Mayflower."

How odd a coincidence that Boughton, who himself painted the Pilgrims, should have been the man to locate what was probably the only accurate representation of what the Pilgrims really looked like. Or perhaps it was the other way round, and Boughton found the Cuyp painting first and it inspired him to paint the Pilgrims.

Whatever happened, he had found one of the lost art treasures of the world. Its value? It would be impossible to judge the value of this particular painting today, but recently a Cuyp painting sold for $71,400.

Yet this was only one of the lost paintings, for there must be many hundreds of them if it were possible to list and catalogue them. The simplest way, of course, to search for lost paintings is to watch for the signature of the artist on any painting which you might find.

To list all of these artists would be impossible without writing a complete book on this subject; but below are a few names of different periods and nationalities, together with some definite lost paintings. Also included are prices of paintings which are not lost but which give some indication of the value of a particular artist's work.

Peter Paul Rubens. A painter whose works bring fabulous prices. Recently one of his paintings sold for $770,000.

Paul Cézanne. One of his paintings recently sold for over $400,000, another for $616,000, and yet another for $252,000.

Vincent van Gogh. One of his paintings sold for almost $400,000.

Edouard Manet. One of his paintings sold for $316,400.

El Greco. One of his paintings sold recently for over $200,000.

Pablo Picasso. One of his paintings sold for $152,000.

Modigliani. One of his paintings recently sold for over $57,000.

George Inness. A painter whose works are always in demand, works which, when discovered, find their places readily in galleries and museums. Already there are five of his paintings in the Metropolitan Museum in New York City.

Edgar Degas. His painting "After The Bath" was stolen from the Milwaukee Art Institute. While it is difficult to appraise this painting, I have seen the value quoted at $6,000.

John Singleton Copley. Recently an estimate of over $2,500 was placed on one of his paintings.

Katsushika Hokusai. A Japanese artist who produced so many paintings that anyone could have one of them without even knowing it, especially since they were so little thought of in his own country that they were used as wrapping paper for exports. If you should find a Hokusai, however, remember that it would have to be in good condition and neither torn nor wrinkled, for it to have any great value.

Evert Duyckinck (the First). An early American painter, ALL of whose works are known to be missing. In this case, however, there is no way of knowing how much value his paintings would have until one has been found and has been appraised by the experts.

Rembrandt van Rijn. Last but by no means least, this great Dutch master's painting "Aristotle Contemplating the Bust of Homer" was recently sold at auction to New York's Metropolitan Museum for $2,300,000!

There is of course no way of telling, for example, that Degas or Rubens or El Greco painted such and such a number of paintings and that such and such a number are now missing. This would be an impossibility, but there is a very good chance that these artists did paint works, especially during their younger and struggling days, that have never been found.

Watch for their signatures on any painting that you find, and, even if you personally do not care for it, remember that the average person is not an art connoisseur. The question of the beauty and fame of a painting rests with the art critics, the museum curators, and the collectors.

Watch especially for the paintings of the Impressionists, works by such masters as Cézanne, Pissarro, Sisler and Renoir. Many years passed before these men were recognized. Their works were laughed at and ridiculed. No one wanted them. No one liked them. No one would buy them. There is no way of telling how many of their paintings were lost because of the little value they had at that time.

Watch for paintings by all of the great masters of the past. That old painting which you thought so little of might turn out to be one of the finest examples of the master's touch the world has ever seen. Tomorrow it might be hanging in the gallery of a famous museum —and you will be out buying your first yacht.

X

ADVENTURE BY PROXY

Barometers, Globes, Figureheads

PEOPLE who normally lead a humdrum existence seem to go wild when confronted with any memento of the days when men went down to the sea in ships and sailed to lands that were still wild and unknown.

Businessmen who look upon their latest "big deals" as an everyday occurrence worth only another twinge from their ulcer become excited at the thought of an ancient globe or antique barometer. For when they buy these things they bring into their modern-day world a small breath of a life that, while it can never come again, will at least never be forgotten.

They clutch at antique barometers, and price, it seems, is no object, if the barometer is rare enough and fine enough. It does not even matter, it seems, whether or not the barometer ever actually went to sea. Sometimes a fine specimen made by a famous furniture designer is worth a great deal even if it never left the shore, like the eighteenth-century barometer which was recently appraised at over $800.

Antique globes can also bring a gleam to the collector's eye. Some of these date as early as the fourteen hundreds. The oldest globe that we have today is one which was made in 1492. It could be that you will be the treasure hunter lucky enough to find a globe made even earlier than this. Or perhaps a globe similar to the Lenox globe, which is today in the New York Public Library. It is one of the earliest known examples to show both hemispheres, and, while this is important in determining its value, the information contained on a globe is not always the most important factor. Sometimes the globe together with the stand upon which it rests is valuable because of the furniture maker who designed it, such as the Sheraton globe which was made about the early eighteen hundreds and which was valued at $650.

Globes that are very old, globes that have erroneous information on them, and globes that were designed by names famous in early furniture design are all worth watching for, just as anything connected with the sea is worth watching for. Even a jug with Admiral Nelson's portrait on it can be worth around $20 or $30.

Anything connected with the sea can be of value, although sometimes the item cannot be measured in terms of money. Often a treasure find is measured in terms of historical value far more than monetary value. There was, for example, the man who went on a picnic and found a part of an object that belongs to history.

It is the story of a young man who went on a picnic with the sole purpose of finding relaxation away from the sprawling city of San Francisco. Far from the big city, in the rolling hills and rocky shore of Marin County, California, the young man laughed and joked with his friends, glad, for once, to be away from the dust and grime of everyday living that is the focus around which city life revolves.

He and his friends gathered up the picnic things when they were ready to go home, and they all piled into the young man's car.

As they were driving along the busy highway they soon discovered that one of the car's tires had developed a flat.

They fixed the tire, and, when they were finished, the young man took another minute to climb the bluff along the road. He looked down at the pounding Pacific below; then he turned back toward his friends, only to stumble against something that was almost completely buried in the dirt of the hillside.

He picked it up and glanced at it casually. It was a piece of time-blackened metal with an odd round hole in it. As he started to throw it away he felt the soundness of the metal between his thumb and forefinger, and he shrugged and decided to keep it. Maybe his old car could use a piece of metal in its innards some day.

He took the piece of metal home with him, threw it into a corner of his garage, and forgot about it for many months—until the time came when the car broke down again.

Metal! He needed a piece of metal! He was just about to go to the junkyard when he remembered the piece of metal he had picked up on the bluff near the ocean on the day of the picnic.

It was dirty, so he picked up a work rag and began to clean away the blackness. "What an odd hole in it," he thought, noticing again the strange, circular cut-out in the metal.

It took quite a while, but finally he could see that part of the black was disappearing. Then he noticed that there was something on the metal. He took it over to the light, and, examining it carefully, he made out the letters of a name—Francis Drake.

The youth was not too sure of what he had, but he knew enough to take the piece of metal to the proper authorities. Today that piece of metal, once intended for use in a young man's car, is the honored property of the University of California.

It is known to historians as "Drake's Plate," left by Drake as a marker claiming the land for Elizabeth I of England, and naming the land New Albion.

But not all of the plate has yet been found. What about the circular hole in the plate? Within that hole, Francis Drake had placed an English sixpence bearing Her Majesty's portrait. Somehow, through the centuries, the coin became separated from the plate, and today, somewhere along the coast of the Pacific Ocean, in Marin County, California, is an English six-penny piece that will fit the hole in Drake's Plate.

If you could find this sixpence, it would be one of the treasure finds of the decade—at least in terms of historical value.

IN the days when it took months to cross the ocean and each port was an adventure, a ship became a man's second home and he was as proud of her as though she were his sweetheart.

In his effort to show what he felt about her he placed figures on her bow, figures of many things: of women, statesmen, animals, dolphins, legendary figures, and even alligators.

Today these ships' figureheads can be worth as much as $2,000 to $3,000 apiece. These huge, symbolic figures which have disappeared from the world of ships can take their places in today's museums—at a price that makes it worth the while of any treasure hunter to look for them. For every old ship that sailed the sea there was a figurehead, and today there are many hundreds of them which have never been found. Among these missing figureheads is that of the ship "Columbus," the figurehead representing its name-sake, Christopher Columbus.

A long time ago a group of cadets at the U.S. Naval Academy were watching a minstrel show which rang with songs and jokes good enough to make the young students roar with laughter. High-light of the evening, however, came when the minstrels rolled out a figure which was more than well known to the cheering students.

It did not look like much, with one shoulder broken and the ruff partially gone, the paint showing the effects of the wind-swept storms of the sea, for this was the proud if battered figurehead of the Columbus.

It had known history in its day. It had shipped home Canova's figure of Washington. It was at Canton when the United States ne-gotiated the first treaty of peace with China. Stephen Decatur him-self approved a bill to have the carver of the figurehead superintend final work on it. This historic background was one of the reasons why, when the cadets saw the figurehead being rolled forward, they stood up and cheered.

After the evening's entertainment was over, the figurehead, one of the Academy's proudest possessions, had to be put away. It was placed in a shed for safe-keeping—and it disappeared. To this day no one knows what happened to it.

How it came to be at the Academy is a story in itself, for, during the days of the Civil War, the Columbus was berthed at the city of Norfolk at a time when the city fathers were certain that the Con-federates were close enough to capture their ships. So they burned them and one of the ships partially destroyed by their own hand was the Columbus. Yet the figurehead itself survived. We do not know if it was removed from the ship before the ship was burned; we know only that it did survive the fire.

From here it traveled to the Boston Navy Yard, and finally to the Naval Academy. And now it has disappeared.

The Columbus figurehead survived many things, even the burn-ing of the ships at Norfolk, but there were many other figureheads in the fire that day and one of them was a figurehead representing Hercules on the ship "Pennsylvania."

The Hercules was not just another figurehead but was the last work by the great figurehead carver William Rush. Knowing that death was imminent he asked only that he be allowed to carve the Hercules for the Pennsylvania. In deference to a dying man's wish he was recommended for the job and got it.

Rush carved the Hercules almost as he lay dying, and it is this Hercules which is missing today. It has been suggested that it was destroyed in the Norfolk fire. Perhaps! And perhaps it was saved like the Columbus! If so, then perhaps you can find it.

Look for it in the junkyards, the lumber yards, and the antique shops. These are the places where you would be most likely to find any missing ship's figurehead—all but one of them, anyway.

This is the figurehead of the whaling ship "Rebecca." The figurehead is, of all things, buried in the sands at New Bedford, Massachusetts, a city which is famous for its connections with the history of the sea. In former times it was a famous port of entry as well as a center for the whaling trade.

At that time one of New Bedford's latest whaling ships was the "Rebecca," and before she was launched a figurehead was placed on her bow, a figurehead representing the eldest daughter of Joseph Russell, who was one of the founders of New Bedford.

Usually, of course, a figurehead goes through storms and battle and even fire before being taken off its ship, yet this time the ship had not even been launched before the figurehead was taken down.

The owners of the ship were staunch members of the Society of Friends, and they thought the figurehead was an extravagance— in their minds a sinful thing.

Whatever discussions or arguments the rest of the town might have had about the figurehead, the opinions of the owners prevailed and the figurehead was removed. But this was not the end of it, for after its removal some of the younger and more spirited of the male population, including, of all people, the brother of the girl the figurehead depicted, took the figurehead and buried it in the sand.

What an unlikely place to look for a ship's figurehead—yet a treasure can be anywhere at all. And the value can be almost anything.

Some figureheads are worth a great deal, and all of them are worth something. There is no guarantee, of course, that the above figureheads are worth the $2,000 or $3,000 mentioned before. It would depend entirely on their condition, and on how much collectors wanted them.

ILLUSTRATIONS

18 to 25

18. St. John Nepomuk by an anonymous New Mexico folk artist, whose working dates were 1809-1830. This panel, painted in tempera over gesso on pine, measures 6 x 3½ inches. It disappeared from the storage area of the Museum of New Mexico in July, 1957. *(Ch. XVI)*

19. Page One of *The Boston News-Letter*, Number 1, April 17 to 24, 1704. Only three copies of this paper are known to be extant—a rare find if another can be located. (*Ch. XVII*)

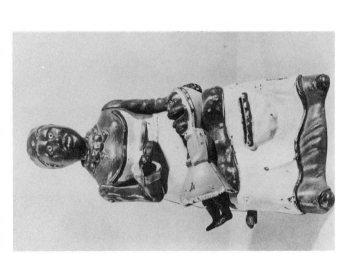

20. Left: a child's bank, "Mammy and Child," patented October 1884. The coin is placed on the spoon in the mother's hand and "fed" into the child's mouth. When lever is pressed, child kicks its feet, Mammy nods her head and feeds the baby with the spoon. This bank has another coin entrance in the mother's apron. Right: "Uncle Sam" bank, patented June 1886. This, a typical American bank, includes a carpet bag which opens when lever is pressed. The coin, placed in Uncle Sam's extended hand falls into the bag; at the same time his whiskers move. (Ch. XVIII)

21. Top: child's bank, "Eagle and Eaglets," patented January 1883, originally called "American Eagle Bank." Coin is deposited from bill of the mother bird into the nest; mother bird's wings flap and the eaglets open their mouths and "chirp" for their food. This chirping is made by a bellows in the mechanism. Center: "Magician Bank" patented January 1882. Magician stands before a table upon which the coin is placed. Pressing a lever causes him to lower his hat over the coin; he nods his head and the coin disappears. Bottom: "Always Did 'Spice a Mule" patented August 1879. Boy, coin in lap, is seated on a bench facing the mule. When the spring is released the mule turns completely around and kicks the boy over the bench backwards; coin falls into base under the bench. (Ch. XVIII)

22. A fifty-dollar bill issued by the Republic of Texas (1836-1845). These bills, issued in denominations from $1 to $500 are today worth from $20 to $500. Below, the famous 1804 silver dollar has been sold at auctions in excess of $28,000. (*Ch. XIX*)

Courtesy of John J. Ford, Jr.

23. Fine example of a Persian silk rug. It has silver and silk background, Ghiordes knot. The all over symmetrical pattern is predominately apricot and green, with touches of light and medium blues. (Ch. XX)

Courtesy of The Smithsonian Institution, from the Clara W. Berwick Collection

24. A page from the Gutenberg Bible, one of the world's most famous books. (Ch. XXI)

25. "The Four Horsemen of The Apocalypse" by Albrecht Dürer. Note the famous Dürer monogram, the A over D, at the bottom of the work. Watch for very old etchings or woodcuts bearing this monogram. *(Ch. XXII)*

This is true of any kind of treasure, but, if you should find a ship's figurehead, and it is old enough and in fine enough condition, it is probably worth a great deal, especially if the ship it decorated was important historically.

One thing to remember in looking for figureheads is that it is possible that the arms are separate from the body. They were made that way so that the arms could be removed in case of a storm, because the arms were easily damaged by rough weather.

But find a figurehead and all its parts and you may have found something worth about four figures.

XI

THE GREATEST TREASURE OF THEM ALL

The Story of the Holy Grail

IT is the year 1910, near the world-famous city of Antioch in Syria. Workmen labor at the digging of a well, and, as the work proceeds, the piles of dirt taken out of the ground grow higher and higher.

Suddenly the work stops, as one of the workmen spots a gleam of metal shining in the sunlight. Carefully he and his companions remove it from the surrounding dirt.

As they scrape away the centuries-old crusty residue, they find that they have unearthed two cups, one set within the other. The inner cup is very plain and unprepossessing, but the outer cup is made of silver.

The cups pass out of their hands and into the possession of the experts. Slowly the word spreads, and museum curators and historians from all over turn their eyes toward the two cups, for now the word is out that perhaps here, near the city of Antioch, in the year of Our Lord one thousand nine hundred and ten, the greatest treasure of them all has been found. For it is believed that the inner cup might be that most fabulous of all treasures—the Holy Grail!

The experts argued and examined and tested, and for a long time the only thing upon which they agreed at all was to disagree. Certainly the legends of the Holy Grail bore out the possibility of the finding of the cup somewhere near Antioch, for almost immediately after the Last Supper the cup had passed out of the hands of Christ and into the possession of Joseph of Arimathea.

It is said that Joseph caught in this cup the blood that flowed from Christ's wounds as he was dying. The legend goes on to tell of the miraculous transportation of Joseph to England—and with him went the Grail, which ever after was miraculously filled with food and drink for Joseph.

Then for many centuries the stories of the Grail are concerned mainly with men's attempt to find it. The Knights of the Round Table made the search for the Grail a part of their chivalric code. Everyone knows the story of Galahad, the pure in heart, who saw the Grail.

Certainly, aside from these legends, there seems to be a good foundation for the idea that the Grail was taken to England by Joseph of Arimathea. The legend of the Grail was known in West Britain even before the days when the inhabitants were converted to Christianity.

But after Galahad? What happened to it then? According to the legend, the Crusaders actually had the Grail. With it in their possession they marched toward the Holy Land, and one of their purposes was to once more replace the Grail in the land from whence it originally came.

Yet their hopes were greater than their fortunes, because they were both outnumbered and outfought. But even in defeat their thought was of the Grail. Rather than let it fall into the hands of the enemy they buried it—near Antioch.

And it was here that the workmen dug their well and unearthed the cup that for a while excited every museum curator in the world. It was a lovely cup, too, even though when cleaned it was found to be damaged by corrosion. It was cleaned by the finest experts in the field, and today it is a lovely object. The inner cup is very plain, but the outer cup is of chased silver portraying vines and figures and grapes, all of them woven into an artistic setting which is still lovely even after all the centuries it lay in dust and dirt.

Today, this cup is in the possession of the Metropolitan Museum in New York City and it can be seen there at any time. It is called the "Antioch Chalice," because, unfortunately for the world but fortunately for the treasure hunter, it has been finally decided that this cup is *not* the Holy Grail.

It took exhaustive tests, a great deal of research, and the varied opinions of many many experts before this decision was finally reached, but today the authorities of the Metropolitan Museum of Art reject the theory that it is the Grail.

They list the age of the Antioch Chalice as being of the fourth or possibly fifth century, very early Christian work certainly, but they deny that the inner cup is the one out of which Jesus actually drank.

If this then is not the Holy Grail, then the Grail is still among the missing treasures of the world. One cannot imagine the price which men could ask for this holiest of all the drinking cups of the ages!

Yet, certainly, the finding of the Grail would have much more far-reaching effects than the monetary reward it might bring, for this is the cup to which the knights of the Middle Ages dedicated their whole lives, the cup for which the crusaders gave their lives.

This is the cup which, if found, would bring into actuality the legends which have followed its existence for almost two thousand years.

For this is the cup out of which Christ drank at the Last Supper. It stood on the same table where Christ broke bread with his Apostles. This is the cup that has been searched for by more people than any other lost treasure in the world.

There is no museum curator, no expert, no historian who could turn his back on it—if you could find it.

For now, after the original excitement of the finding of the Antioch Chalice, after the disappointment when it was finally determined that it was not the Holy Grail, the experts are more aware than ever that someday the Grail may still be found.

And until the day comes, the Holy Grail must remain the most important lost treasure in the world.

XII

TREASURE IN THE JUNKYARD

Carriages, Coaches, and Cars

PEDESTRIANS watched breathlessly as the strange-looking vehicle came hurtling down the road like a juggernaut of fantastic speed. Missing the now screaming onlookers by inches, the vehicle hurtled toward a brick wall. Nothing could stop the inevitable. Unable to come to a halt, the vehicle plunged into the brick wall—and the wall tumbled down.

Police arrived on the scene and, as usual in these cases, argument and discussion ensued with voices raised loud and anger rampant. The man had been speeding—of this the police were certain. But they were not as sure of themselves and of their laws against speeding as policemen of today would be—for this was the year 1769.

The vehicle, which was probably the first one ever involved in the misdemeanor of speeding, is lost. It would be, if you could find it today, one of the greatest finds in the history of antique-car treasure hunting.

Made by Captain Cugnot in 1769, it would be an historic find in this field, similar in value, possibly, to the steam artillery-carriage made a year later in 1770 by this same Captain Cugnot, a man undaunted by his previous set-to with the law.

Today the steam artillery-carriage is in the *Conservatoire National des Arts et Métiers* in Paris, France, an historic relic of the world's automotive past. But Cugnot's other car? It is one of the most fabulous missing automobile treasures.

Many early vehicles like Cugnot's steam artillery-carriage, however, are in museums and collections. In the United States National Museum is the first successful gasoline car built in America. Conceived by one brother and built by another, this vehicle is an American first. It was Charles E. Duryea who conceived the idea for the car, and his brother, J. Frank Duryea, who built it.

In the *Deutsches Museum* in Munich, Germany, there is a vehicle which owed its existence to two men. It is a three-wheeler built in 1885 by Carl Benz with an engine by Gottlieb Daimler, the man who developed the high-speed gasoline power plant which Benz used in the three-wheeler.

One inventor in this category of extant cars had great hopes for his machine. He called it *L'Obeissante* which means, of course, the Obedient. This was the steam coach built in 1873 by Amédée Bollec. This coach is now in the *Conservatoire National,* Paris.

In the Henry Ford Museum in Dearborn, Michigan, is a steam buggy made during the Civil War period by Sylvester H. Roper.

There are many, many of these rare examples in museums today, but there are others, like the 1769 Cugnot vehicle, which have never been found. Coaches belonging to such men as Sir Charles Dance, Maceroni, Summers, J. Scott Russell, and Church, have disappeared. Other men, too, made vehicles which today have gone the way of so many things of the past. The coaches, for example, of both Squire and Ogle have completely disappeared. Not one of these vehicles is known to exist, and they are among the lost treasures of the antique-car field. Find just one of them, and you are on the road to fortune.

Also missing are the coaches of Goldsworthy Gurney; the coaches of Walter Hancock, the man who first made use of the hand brake; and the coaches of W. H. James, famous for his introduction of the variable-ratio transmission. Any of the coaches made by these men would be worth money in your pocket if you could find them.

These missing coaches were English, built between 1820 and 1840. They were steam stagecoaches, on their way to becoming numerous when opposition was raised to them mainly by owners of railroads and conventional stagecoach lines. They simply could not stand the competition from the better steam stagecoaches.

A law was passed—the so-called red-flag law—which insisted, not only that the steam stagecoaches be preceded by a man walking with a red flag in his hand, but that the speed of the coaches be limited to four miles an hour.

So the steam stagecoaches passed from England's roads, but to-day, if you spot one, hang on to it, for these vehicles are among the most sought-after collectors' items in this field.

But do not stop there. Watch for any old car. The one you thought was junk might turn out to be priceless. It is of course hard to place a definite market value on any specific car. The value would depend on age, rarity, condition, and how badly the collectors want it.

Antique-car collecting has become a craze in America in recent years. Our automotive civilization likes to remember its past. There are already some fabulous collections—like the Long Island Automobile Museum, the exhibit at the Museum of Science and Industry in Chicago, the exhibit at the Smithsonian Institution, and the famous Harrah's Collection. The collections grow, and the craze continues.

So take another look at that old car which you saw the other day in your neighborhood junkyard. Maybe it was not just another old car—maybe it was really a collector's item worth a fortune!

HOW much is that old car you saw in the junkyard really worth? It might be worth $5. It might be worth $50. It might be worth $5,000—depending, again, on condition, rarity, make and age.

At least one old car was evaluated at $10,000 by the insurance appraisers. Unhappily for the insurance company who set this evaluation, the car was burnt in a fire that destroyed it while it was on display as an exhibit in the 1929 Los Angeles Auto Show.

This was a 1901 Packard, one of five models which were made that year, models which were all two-passenger cars and had one-cylinder engines and wheel bases of seventy-five inches.

That there were five of these models made we know from the records of the Studebaker-Packard Corporation in South Bend, Indiana. What we do not know is where all of these cars are today. One of them, of course, was the one destroyed in the Auto Show. We also know that several years ago Mr. Henry Joy of Detroit, Michigan, purchased a second 1901 Packard. This leaves three 1901 Packards not accounted for.

They could, of course, already be in the hands of the collectors.

It would be impossible, however, to ascertain this without writing to every museum, every collector, and every old-car enthusiast in the world. Obviously, this would be impossible.

The logical thing would be to simply remember the 1901 Packard and watch for it. That old car which you thought was junk might turn out to be a $10,000 horseless carriage that collectors would give their eye teeth to have.

Any car from the early 1900's is worth checking, and, strangely enough, these cars are not as scarce as most people think. In 1901, the same year as the 1901 Packard, there were 14,800 passenger cars registered in the United States, and each one is a potential missing treasure varying in value from $10 to $10,000, depending of course on rarity and condition.

Not only cars from the early 1900's can be of value—any make of early car can be worth something. There have been so many kinds of cars made in America, over 2,600 kinds, that chances of finding a collector's item are good.

Sometimes these early cars are destroyed and a treasure is lost forever. Sometimes the loss of the car is accidental, as with the 1901 Packard destroyed in the Auto Show.

Sometimes, however, the loss of the car is just plain thoughtlessness—like the car which was used, in the first American automobile race, by Frank Duryea. Duryea made racing history when he won the race, but years later treasure history was also made when the car was junked—a loss to treasure hunters and collectors that can never be replaced.

Sometimes a car may even be destroyed for patriotic reasons. When World War II broke out, the grandson of Alexander Winton, one of our first automobile builders, gave his grandfather's first automobile to the scrap drive—and it was lost forever.

The treasure hunter must never destroy a car or junk it until he knows what it is. What you think is junk might be considered a treasure by the collectors.

Things are being destroyed today which may be of value some day in the future—if they could be preserved. Antique fire engines have been scrapped in countless numbers, because fire departments either sold them or used them for parts long before they reached the antique-car category. Their value would probably be small today, although there are many good specimens already in museums. What they would be worth in the future if they could be preserved, no one knows, but probably a great deal—if you find one and preserve it.

The transportation of the pioneers has also suffered from this thoughtlessness. Conestoga wagons wore out or were left to rot. And on the rivers the early steamboats of the waterway pioneers were left to rot, sold for lumber, or destroyed by unthinking Tom Sawyerish juveniles.

These objects are rapidly disappearing from the scene, to be forgotten forever unless the treasure hunter does something about it. For, if he can stop the destruction, he is on his way to placing examples of an almost forgotten way of life in the hands of the collectors—and money in his pocket.

XIII

It's a Man's World

Guns, Glasses, Knives and Armor

WHEN a man becomes a collector of the old and the rare, he usually becomes more of a fanatic about it than any woman with her antique furniture or her antique glass. And, when he becomes a fanatic, he becomes a buyer of anything old and rare that you can find.

The gentleman collector takes pride in the walls of his den, which are decorated with antique Colts, Smith and Wessons, dueling pistols, and perhaps a curio or two. Gleaming amongst the array of firearms there might also be a circlet of antique daggers from all nations and all centuries.

Even the paintings on the walls will reflect his taste, for they will be of the early days of our old West, and if he is lucky enough he will count a Remington among them.

Perhaps, draped gracefully on one wall, might be a horse trapping and perhaps, if he is fortunate, it might be as lovely a horse trapping as the one which belonged to Lorenzo de Medici—a trapping with embroidered figures of silver thread on a background of blue velvet.

Perhaps there will also be one or two nineteenth-century decoys. Decoys, worth perhaps not more than $30 or $40, but dear to the male collector's heart.

Perhaps the gentleman will make himself more comfortable by

removing his boots on a $25 or $30 bootjack of a kind that goes begging in most second-hand stores.

He will perhaps walk to the mantel, where he displays his collection of Early American snuffboxes. If he is very wealthy, there might be one or two made of precious metals and encrusted with fine gems, or perhaps they will be of shell or exotic woods.

And, if he continues with the collection of items connected with man's desire for snuff and tobacco, he might have books, manuscripts or letters scattered tastefully around the room, all of them connected with the history of the growing of tobacco. If he is lucky enough, he might even have documents equal in historical importance to the first printed accounts of the first bringing of West Indian tobacco seeds into Virginia, such as were on display at the Virginia and Tobacco Show, part of the Arents Collections of the New York Library. Or he might have letters similar to those signed by Elizabeth I of England, which were also a part of the same display.

If he is interested in every aspect of the male animal rather than just his tobacco habit, he might have a collection of shaving mugs, some of them worth forty or fifty dollars apiece. Or, perhaps, if he is very, very lucky, he will have found one particular shaving mug which, as far as we know, is still missing.

The existence of this mug can be deduced from a Currier and Ives print which shows that fabulous showman P. T. Barnum. The same print shows a shaving mug, a mug which would be very valuable if it could be found.

Or he might be more interested in games of chance and have on display cribbage boxes worth around $30 apiece. Or antique playing cards!

Perhaps he will be more interested in the fine old art of drinking, and all along one wall he will have a collection of things connected with this greatest of all indoor sports.

The flag bottles will be displayed a little sideways, so that the viewer can easily see that on one side of the bottle is an American flag with thirteen stars and on the other side the words, "New Granite Glass Works, Stoddard, N.H."

There will be glass flasks from the eighteen hundreds worth from $30 to $40 apiece; fox and fish-head stirrup cups worth sometimes a hundred dollars apiece; very old drinking steins; nineteenth-century Toby jugs worth sometimes a hundred dollars each; or even old pewter tankards worth several hundred dollars apiece.

He might even own an oliphant, a very old drinking horn; some of them date from the Middle Ages.

Perhaps his friends will arrive, and, not only to impress them with his collection, but because they become very gay, he will bring out his matched set of firing glasses, very old glasses made in England during the middle seventeen hundreds.

He will bring out a very old bottle of wine and fill the glasses, remarking on the heavy bases of the glasses, commenting that today most wine glasses are such fragile things.

He will explain carefully that these heavy bases are this way for a reason, a very particular reason. The thing to do first, he explains, is for someone to propose a toast—to the evening, the company, or even perhaps a lovely lady of their acquaintance. A toast is proposed and he raps the table with the heavy base of the glass, telling his guests to follow suit. Shortly, throughout the room, as more and more of the glass bases hit the table, there is a loud and deafening noise similar in sound to the firing of guns—for these are the firing glasses of England, the collector's delight.

But anything this man owns is a delight, for he is a collector. And it is to such men as this that the treasure hunter must cater, for it is to them that he must sell his wares.

Whether it is a gun, a dagger, a snuffbox or a drinking glass—this man will buy it, if you can find it.

I F you can find a Colt Model 1847 (Whitneyville-Walker) revolver that is in good condition, you can collect anything up to $5,000 for it.

Only about a hundred of these guns are extant today. They are the rarest of the guns produced by Samuel Colt, the American whose name is almost synonymous with firearms, and they are worth up to $5,000 apiece if you can find one in good condition.

Any old gun, if it is rare enough and in good enough condition, is worth something on the collectors' market. One of these guns about which we hear so much—in every legend, every movie, every story of the old West—is the Smith and Wesson .44 caliber American revolver.

This is the gun that opened up the frontier. All the way west to California, the Smith and Wesson forged a pathway for the settlers to follow. For this reason alone the gun has great historical value, but it also has a monetary value if you can find one in good condition.

Most of the examples of this gun are in very poor condition, because they were used so much. They were part of the frontiersman's standard equipment. Most of them found today are very much beaten and battered, but find one in good condition and it becomes a collector's item.

Watch for any old gun. There is one type of flintlock which is worth twice its weight in gold—and it weighs four pounds three ounces. This is the United States Model 1799 flintlock pistol. Find one in mint condition, and double its weight in terms of gold.

Strangely enough there were some two thousand of these pistols made; yet today there are less than a dozen known to exist. Everyday arithmetic shows that this leaves one thousand nine hundred and eighty-eight pistols which have not as yet found their way into the hands of the collectors.

True, some, perhaps most, of them will have been destroyed or damaged, but there should be many left which are of great value— to be exact, twice their weight in gold.

Even the old-time blunderbuss can be worth a couple of hundred dollars if it is in fine enough condition. Any kind of old gun is worth investigation, because they are all worth something.

A matched pair of dueling pistols is worth a couple of hundred dollars, and such oddities as a lady's muff pistol can be worth $70 or $80, depending, of course, upon condition.

Condition is the prime factor in determining the value of a gun, but historical importance can also be a determining factor. Of late years collectors have been, more and more, demanding the guns of the frontiersmen and the outlaws of the early west. Find a gun that belonged to a famous outlaw, authenticate it, and you have a collector's item.

When you hear that a collector has a gun that belonged to a certain lawman or outlaw—do not stop looking for the guns of this particular man. These men used many guns during their lifetime, and any of their guns is a collector's item—if you can find it.

Try, however, to authenticate the ownership of the gun as much as possible, since this raises the value of the weapon. Authentication, of course, is not always easy, but it is desirable. And guns are not the only things that have an authenticated history in back of them. For example, R. R. Riss II of New York owns the famous tomahawk that belonged to Daniel Boone, and, equally important, he has affidavits concerning this tomahawk dating back to the year 1898.

The Boone Tomahawk was made by Robert Beaty, and it would be well to remember this name. For anything made by Beaty, who was the first to make edged weapons in the United States, is a rarity.

There are all kinds of daggers and knives which are collectors' items—if you can find them. There are knives of the sixteen hundreds which were decorated with gold and silver and ivory. These are rarities. Very few of these early knives are around today. Probably one of the finest of these early knives still extant is the knife of Louis Le Bon. It is decorated with silver gilt and enamels.

Any knife from the Middle Ages is a collector's item. The knights had knives which they used for battle—their table knives were luxury items. The handles of these table knives were decorated in many different ways, some of them indicating the season of the year, with ivory handles for Easter and ebony handles for Lent.

These knives of the Middle Ages are, of course, becoming more and more scarce as time goes on—and therefore more valuable. Anything from this period should be watched for. As, for example, any of the armor of this time.

Armor of the Middle Ages is getting more rare with every passing year, and every piece of it which you can find in good condition is a collector's item. It is getting so scarce of late that not even antique dealers see suits of armor for long periods of time.

If you can find any of these items—the guns, the knives, the armor—the market is wide open, since collectors are becoming more numerous every year. The collecting of arms and armor, of course, has been popular for centuries. In the early fifteen hundreds, Louis XII collected arms and armor. In more recent days, one man, William Henry Riggs, collected more than two thousand five hundred separate pieces.

The market, as stated, is wide open. Your only problem is to find a rare item in good condition. Then you can start collecting what may very well turn out to be a small fortune.

❧ ⚜ ☙

XIV

MINIATURES TO GIANTS

The Smallest and the Largest Art Treasures

THE lost art treasures of the world take many forms: huge giants of the sculptor's world, fine and delicate glass of the Venetian period, fine woods of antique furniture, magnificent tapestries. They come in every form under the sun, but probably one of the smallest items would be the miniature paintings made before the advent of the modern camera.

Today our photographic equipment records, with very little trouble and with absolute accuracy, whatever is placed in front of it, but in the days of yore only the artist could do this. Yet members of families wanted a record of their loved ones, and, huge paintings or wall portraits not always being practical, the miniature came into popularity.

The miniature became a well loved and common thing in the average home, and today these miniatures, or at least those by certain artists, are sought eagerly by collectors. The collecting of miniatures has, rightly, become almost a fad in America today, and the number of men and women collecting these small paintings is increasing every day; and, as their number increases, the competition for works by specific artists will become more profitable, so the treasure hunter who finds a rare miniature will be able almost to name his own price.

Many of these miniatures were made during the seventeen hundreds in America, as they were extremely popular. Today no one knows how many of them are missing, or how many of them are hiding in that famous old trunk in your attic or in that box of odds and ends in the basement.

There are, however, certain artists whose works are more highly valued than just any early artist, and among these men is Charles Willson Peale, who is probably better remembered for his portrait of George Washington which today hangs in the National Gallery in Washington, D.C.

Peale was well known even in his own day, having commanded a company of soldiers during some of the most famous battles of the Revolutionary War. He painted many, many portraits, among them miniatures which rank, today, as choice items on the collector's list.

Another name to watch for is that of John Singleton Copley, whose works are today's museum pieces, his larger paintings being classed among the finest works of American art. But the treasure hunter has more than a good chance of finding a Copley miniature, since they were small and therefore easily lost or mislaid.

Also watch for the signatures of such men as Pelham, Trott, and Fraser. Any miniature by any of these men is a find for the treasure hunter.

From an earlier day, watch for the European miniatures of Holbein, Samuel Cooper, Smart, Robertson, and Ross. Lucas Cranach the Elder also did some miniatures which were exquisite then and are rare collectors' items today.

Also watch for miniatures which were made shortly before the French Revolution, for at that time the art of miniature painting in France, as in America, reached a height of popularity which has not been equaled since. From this period, look for the names of Mausson, Mosnier, and Hall, the latter having been such a magnificent painter of miniatures that he was nicknamed the "Van Dyke of the Miniature."

But there are other miniatures besides those, because miniatures have been a favorite in homes for many, many years. There are miniatures on ivory, canvas, wood, and metal. And all of them, if they are old enough, rare enough, and painted by great artists, have a value to the treasure hunter. Even eighteenth-century French vanity boxes were occasionally decorated with miniature paintings.

Sometimes miniatures were of other subjects than portraits, which is what we generally think of when discussing miniatures. There have been some which were landscapes, although they were

ILLUSTRATIONS

26 to 33

Courtesy of The Corning Museum of Glass

26. Left: tumbler, or flip glass, probably 3rd quarter of 18th century, attributed to the Manheim, Pa., glass works of Henry William Stiegel. Right: also attributed to Stiegel, the "Valentine," or "Betrothal," tumbler is one of the three recorded early American enameled pieces bearing an English inscription. (*Ch. XXIV*)

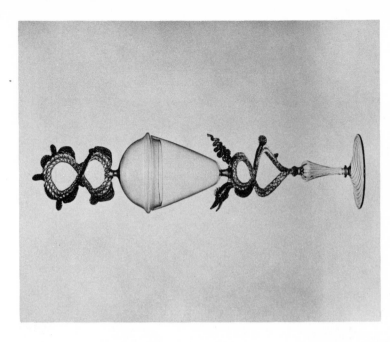

27. Left: Venetian goblet made in the first quarter of the 16th century. It is of clear colorless glass, mold and free blown, tooled with applied parts, gilt and enameled. Right: another 16th-century Venetian goblet is made of soda-lime glass, colorless of yellowish smoky tinge, red and white twists, blue-green trim. It is 8⅞ inches high; with cover it reaches 14 inches. (Ch. XXIV)

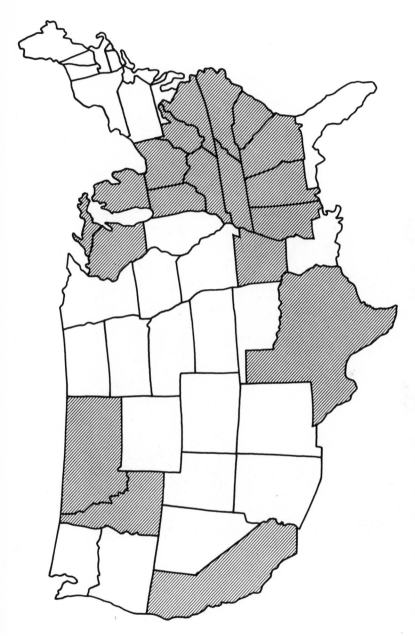

28. Map shows the diamond areas in the United States. There may be more states where diamonds can be found, but the map shows only the finds "officially" recorded. (*Ch. XXVII*)

29. Mementos of early American fire-fighting days. Note especially the "Firemark," the six-pointed star, mounted on a wooden board. This and similar firemarks are extremely rare today and are collectors' items. (*Ch. XXVIII*)

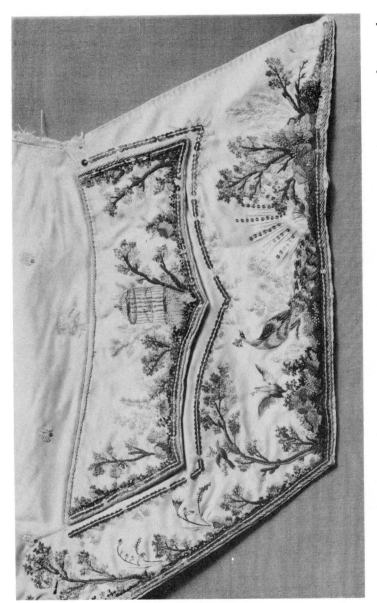

Courtesy of The Metropolitan Museum of Art, Rogers Fund, 1909

30. Fine example of French embroidery of the time of Louis XV (1710-1774). This is a detail of a waistcoat showing the area around the left pocket with an embroidered scene. (*Ch. XXIX*)

31. A pair of silver goblets by Paul Revere, 1782. Works by this famous American silversmith are today eagerly sought by collectors. *(Ch. XXX)*

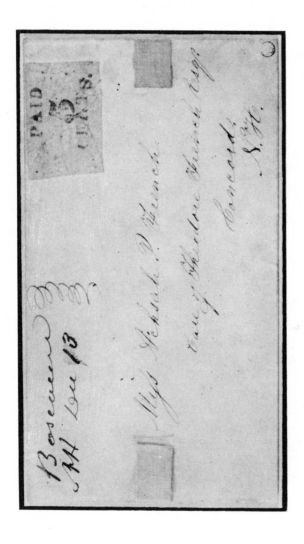

32. A Boscawen, New Hampshire, stamp, one of the most unique of all the Postmasters' Provisionals. Stamps of this type are in great demand today. (*Ch. XXXI*)

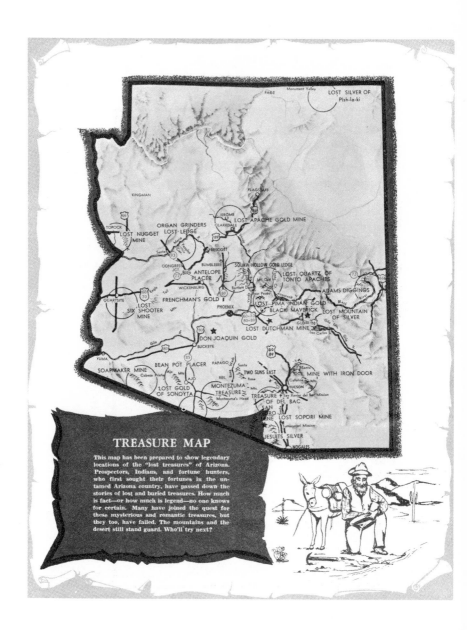

33. "Treasure Map" shows the legendary locations of the "lost treasures" of Arizona. The looking for lost treasures is usually encouraged by the localities in question, and authorities are most cooperative in any research regarding these treasures. *(Ch. XXXIII)*

Courtesy of the State of Arizona Development Board

114

fewer in number than the portrait miniatures. Still they are well worth watching for.

Some of the greatest and most famous artists in the world painted miniatures, and they belong in museums and collections. What a shame it would be if, perhaps, one of the finest examples of this almost lost art should remain in a dusty box in your attic, when with a little searching you might be able to give it back to the world—at the same time making money in the process.

Like petite works of art, these miniatures belie their size and can be placed, both in terms of beauty and of line, beside the greatest works of art. They are warm, magnificent examples of what great artists could do when they painted small items, as opposed to the great murals which they also executed. Though small, they can easily match the great murals in beauty if not in size.

There is, of course, no way of telling how many of these miniatures are lost, nor of telling where they might be. They could be anywhere, even spread all the way across America. In the pioneer days, the people would often take along their miniatures on their way west, when all their other belongings had to be left behind.

It would even be possible to find a miniature by one of the European masters such as Holbein or Cranach the Elder in a West Coast second-hand store, it having been brought across an ocean, a mountain range, and a prairie, in a day when only the smallest items were carried across the land of death and Indians.

Possible? Yes, very much so—for this is the treasure hunter's dream. And sometimes it comes true.

AND then there are the giants!

For over a thousand years art lovers have spoken of and dreamed of the lost statue of Hermes by the Greek master Praxiteles. Somewhere in the mists of time, the statue had disappeared completely. Only whispers of its existence remained, whispers which told of a statue so beautiful that it was outstanding even in the day when it was first made, and this was in the century, 400 to 300 B.C., when Greek sculpture was going through one of its finest periods.

Pausanias, the Greek writer of the second century A.D., described the statue—for he saw it. He said that it was a marble statue of Hermes, magnificent in line and proportion. Hermes held on one arm the baby Dionysius, and in one hand he held a bunch of grapes. This is what we knew from his description, and this is probably all we would ever have known except for a group of German excavators who were working at Olympia in the year 1877.

These men accomplished what the art world had thought impossible. After a thousand years, they found the lost statue of Hermes.

They found it as Pausanias had described it—almost. For time had done its work well. The right arm and the grapes which held it were missing. The left foot and the lower part of the legs were missing. Yet most of the statue was in good condition, a triumphant end to a treasure hunt that had lasted for over a thousand years.

But of the work of Praxiteles the statue of Hermes was the lesser prize, for his greatest work is still listed as missing. This is the statue of Aphrodite, which the ancient world acclaimed as Praxiteles' finest work.

We know it existed, because the Greek author Lucian saw the statue at Cnidus circa 150 B.C. He recorded the fact that he had seen it, and so we know it was there. As Pausanias recorded his visit to Hermes, so Lucian told of his visit to Aphrodite, and so we know they were there. But with Aphrodite's statue we have a further concrete clue not only to its existence but to what it looked like, for there was a coin struck during the ancient days which bore the form of Praxiteles' statue of Aphrodite.

If this Aphrodite could be found, the museums of the world would be more than eager for it, and thousands of art lovers the world over would make journeys to see it; much as in the day when the statue was first created, when the people made pilgrimages to it by the thousands.

Day after day, the people visited this fabulous statue not only because it was Praxiteles' finest work but because the statue was at Cnidus, the town which was supposed to be especially favored by the goddess Aphrodite.

Certainly, this statue would be a find for any treasure hunter. The Hermes is thought to be the only authentic original work of Praxiteles in existence today, but Praxiteles created sixty other works of art, none of which have been located.

But of all his works, the Aphrodite is the one dreamed of, both by the museum curator and the treasure hunter.

Praxiteles, of course, was not the only Greek artist whose works are lost. Among the best known of the other masters whose works have never been found is Lysippus who lived during the time of Alexander the Great.

Lysippus was so well thought of and his works were held in such high esteem that Alexander would allow no other artist to make a statue of him, and one of these statues of Alexander, showing him with a lance in his hand, is missing. But this is only one statue; Lysippus created over one thousand five hundred works of art—yet not a one of his works remains.

His Zeus which was at Tarentum has disappeared; Opportunity, which was at the gates of a temple, has vanished; his gigantic statue of Hercules has been lost. What has happened to these and all the other numerous works he produced we do not know. There is some possibility, of course, that they may have been destroyed, but the probability is that at least some of them have survived.

We know that one of his statues was destroyed. This was the Heracles which was taken from Tarentum to Rome, then finally transported to Constantinople where it was preserved until the eleventh century, when it was melted down.

This may have happened to his other works; yet it is highly unlikely. Fifteen hundred works of art simply do not disappear! They may be lost for a while. Some of them may have been damaged. But somewhere the statues of Lysippus are waiting under the dust of centuries for the treasure hunter to find them.

It takes, of course, a great deal of time and effort to search for and locate such works as these, for they are the works of the very ancient past, a past which is so far away from us that we can only look back upon it with a mingled feeling of awe and respect.

But certainly the search for this type of treasure could be well worth the time and trouble. Old records must be searched; experts must be consulted; digging must be careful and accurate. If you dig for doubloons and the spades and shovels knock them around, no damage has been done, but the careless handling of digging equipment when searching for lost works of art can cause irreparable damage.

This all sounds, and is, very complicated and not the sort of thing for the average treasure hunter, but there is always the chance, the one-in-a-million chance, that you will find one of these treasures in the neighborhood second-hand store or in an old packing crate. Anywhere at all!

XV

THE CAVALRY CHARGE

A Lost Painting by Remington

THERE is a lost painting depicting a cavalry charge, about which there is so much mystery that it is a wonder that it can even be written about as a missing treasure. Yet we have a photograph of it.

No one, that we know of, has ever seen the painting. No one knows where the painting is now. No one knows how it disappeared, or when it disappeared. No one knows exactly when or where the painting was executed. No one knows the exact size of the painting.

Yet it is one of the lost treasures of the art world.

When the personal papers of Frederic Remington, the great artist of the old West, were scrutinized, a photograph was found—a photograph showing a painting of a cavalry charge.

Typically, as if charging right out of a television or movie screen, the cavalrymen present a heroic appearance. The officers are waving sabres and Colt revolvers, the soldiers are brandishing their rifles. Like any Hollywood group of Western extras, they are wearing Stetsons and the inevitable kerchiefs around their necks.

There are other items in the photograph besides this painting, but the painting overshadows everything else—because this painting is by the master Remington who put the history of the early West onto canvas.

Remington knew the West. He lived there, working with the cow-boys, and once actually lived with a group of friendly Indians. He also served with the United States Army in their troubles with those Indians who had not yet succumbed to the superior forces of the white man.

When Remington painted his people of the old West, he knew what he was doing; he painted them as they lived, worked and fought.

This quality is evident in the painting of the cavalry charge, and the experts agree. They have labeled the work as an authentic Remington, a painting fine enough to make the old West live again.

As far as we know, no one has ever seen it, but we know what it looked like because of the photograph. No one knows how it disappeared. We do not know when it was painted, but logically it must have been sometime between 1880, the year Remington began painting, and 1909, the year he died.

It is thought to be a large painting, approximately ten by six feet. Certainly too large to be missed if you do run across it. And if you do find it, there is a buyer for it. The Old Sunny Brook Distillery Co. flatly state that they not only want the painting but that they are willing to pay $25,000 for it.

They state, "we want this picture for use in our advertising and promotional work, which utilizes the paintings of Frederic Remington as illustrations."

For many years this company has shown Remingtons in their advertising. If the painting can be found, the company wishes to use it as "a focal point of a traveling exhibit of Remingtons."

Shortly after Sunny Brook Whiskey announced their offer of a reward for the lost Remington, hundreds of letters started pouring in; each clue was followed, yet no trace of the painting could be found.

The company continues to follow every new lead. One of them, eventually, might be the clue that leads them to the Remington painting—which even now might be in your attic.

If you think you have the Remington, do not send the painting to the company. Take a photograph of it, and write to the Old Sunny Brook Art Jury, Room 1100, 99 Park Avenue, New York 16, N.Y., enclosing the photo. It will be submitted to a panel of experts headed by Harold McCracken, authority on Remington and curator of the Whitney Museum for Western Paintings, at Cody, Wyoming. If the snapshot you submit is judged likely to be of the missing painting, the painting will be inspected. If it is then judged to be the missing painting and in good condition, they will pay you $25,000 for it.

It is possible, according to the company, that the painting may be worth more than $25,000; it may be worth $30,000 or even $50,000! If you wish, the panel of art experts who judge the work will submit it on your account to art galleries and interested buyers for the highest bidding.

If they offer more than the company's guaranteed $25,000 you will be free to sell the picture without any claim by the company, except for use of the picture in their advertising. You will receive the full purchase price, but will have no claim on the company.

With an offer like this, you cannot lose! So take another look in your attic, in your basement, and in the neighborhood second-hand store, where it could be hanging on the walls with a price tag of only a few dollars on it. If you can find it, the painting could be worth as much as $50,000 to you.

XVI

FOR THE GLORY OF GOD

Religious Treasures

WHEN the tomb of the great King Charlemagne was opened in the twelfth century, he was found sitting upright, completely attired in his imperial regalia like a ghost sovereign holding sway over an empire of dust and decay.

But the emperor was not the only thing they found, for in his tomb they discovered a fabulous reliquary, set with sapphires and allegedly containing a piece of the "true cross." The reliquary had rested there quietly for centuries, until 1804, when one of the most beautiful women in Europe visited the tomb at Aix-la-Chapelle. Joséphine de Beauharnais took one look at the reliquary and wanted it.

There was consternation among the treasure keepers of the tomb, but Napoléon Bonaparte insisted and, reluctantly, the keepers gave the reliquary to Joséphine. Where this reliquary is today is a mystery, although rumor has it that it is now in the hands of a French collector. If this is true then it does not belong on the treasure hunter's list. But there were other reliquaries made by the order of Charlemagne which really belong on the treasure hunter's list—for they are missing, completely lost to the world.

Among them are the twenty-four alphabet reliquaries, each of them encrusted with precious gems and each designed for a different letter of the alphabet. The last trace we have of these reliquaries is in the eleventh century, when the so-called "A of Charlemagne," the first of the reliquaries, belonged to a Church in Conques.

Since then, there is no trace of them, and not even the Vatican has any knowledge of the letters. Tiffany's in New York relegates them to the world of legend. Gump's in San Francisco has no information on them. Nor does the College of St. Albert the Great, Dominican House of Studies for the Province of the Holy Name, in Oakland, have any information.

They have become lost even to the historians, but, if you could find even one of the letters, it would be listed as one of the greatest religious treasures found in the last century. They could be anywhere —even in your attic here in America—for when the priests came to this country they brought with them as many of their treasures as they could.

It would not be incredible at all to find one of these reliquaries decorating the altar of some small church in one of America's backwaters. Or one may be in that old trunk in your basement which contains the souvenirs of an ancestor who had been to sea and collected many strange things in even stranger ports.

Or, perhaps, you might find a different reliquary there—even though it might not be one of the twenty-four reliquaries of Charlemagne. Numerous reliquaries were made in the time of the early Christian church, reliquaries made with loving care and decorated with the most costly materials and gems which the artisans could find. For these were the caskets which contained the relics of their saints—sometimes a bone or a fingernail or a piece of hair. Or sometimes even a piece of wood which was allegedly a piece of the "true cross."

These reliquaries were made in many forms, and one of these forms was that of a cross. Since these altar reliquaries were made to hold the relics of their saints, the churches made them with the finest workmanship and costliest gems—each of them a treasure—if you could find it.

There are, of course, reliquaries in the museums today, but there were so many made that there is no way of knowing, since the records are so vague, how many are missing. It is simpler to remember just what reliquaries are and to watch for them.

Remember also that there are so many objects in the world of religion to watch for, because it was here, in the church, where people poured out their hopes and dreams—and in so doing produced some of the world's most beautiful art.

Specialized works of art were also produced, eagerly desired by collectors. From twelfth-century Byzantine art, watch for the Black Virgins: art representing the Virgin Mary with her skin painted black to show her sorrow.

The color black, though again associated with lost religious treasures, is not always associated with sorrow. From the Middle ages watch for representations of Jesus clothed in black garments. Black in this case means death—death to evil. How many of these black Virgins or black Christs were made, or how many are missing, no one knows. One thing, however, is certain: they will be bought by museums—if you can find them.

They could be anywhere. Treasures travel to fantastic places—sometimes right under your nose if you only know what you are looking for. It is to be hoped, of course, that, if you should find a lost religious treasure, it would be in fine condition, for this is important in evaluating any item.

This demand for fine condition also holds true for the wax figures of the saints made during the feudal ages—if you can find them. It also holds true for the stained-glass windows of Europe which even in the tenth century were used to beautify the houses of God.

Stained-glass windows previous to the twelfth century were brilliant in their colors, but by the twelfth century the monks of the Cistercian order issued proclamations to the effect that the violent color of the windows must be subdued.

This edict greatly influenced the creation of stained-glass windows throughout all of Europe, and, in the fourteenth century, there was another stoppage to the making of fine stained-glass windows. This was that medieval phenomenon which was rightly called the Black Death.

The somber churches of the Middle Ages with their vastness and their feeling of immensity possibly needed the glory and brilliancy that comes from a sunbeam slanting through the rich purples and violets of these paintings done in glass.

Any of these fabled windows from any of these centuries is worth watching for, and while there may be little chance of finding a piece or a whole portion of a stained-glass window, still the treasures are there to be found. What museum would not want a fine rainbow-hued window from the Middle Ages?

Think it impossible to find a stained-glass window in America? What, then, of the millionaire California gold-rush miners who shipped treasure here by the wagonload—and then lost it. Or the show-off business tycoons of the '20's who bought treasure by the boatload when most of them did not even know art when they saw it. And many lost it after the crash of '29. Even a stained-glass window could be anywhere in America—if you only bother to look for it. And if you find a religious treasure—of fine craftsmanship and in fine condition—you have something which collectors and museum curators will pay for.

TO the experts a bulto means a carved figure or a figure representing the Madonna, the Christ or the Saints. To the experts a retablo means a religious painting done on wood or skin. To the experts these are examples of very primitive art done in the lands south of the border by the peons. But to the treasure hunter they are lost treasures well worth searching for.

It all began when the conquistadores marched with heavy feet across the lands to the south of us, and the priests of the church went with them. The spilling of blood and the awareness of a new kind of God walked hand in hand.

As early as the fifteen hundreds, the people were helping to decorate their churches. The works of art which they created are to all purposes the art of the people themselves. No Raphaels or da Vincis here, but poor, uneducated people with a need to display their great love for their Church.

Many of these unknown artists were Indians, sometimes of mixed blood, and it was to these people that the Church looked for much of its art. Their works were simple, yet filled with the grandeur of their beliefs. They, from all parts of the Latin countries in our hemisphere, created works of art for the missions, the churches, the schools.

There was no building of religious significance which they did not beautify in some way. No matter how poor the people were, they glorified the Church. They spilled what wealth they had into its paintings, its statues and its decorations. They made bultos and retablos, altar pieces, wood panels, and crucifixes.

Part of this art has survived. Much has disappeared and may today lie forgotten in some peon's hut or even in the home of some American who traveled into the lands of the south and purchased some items from the "natives." Not knowing the value of what they had, it is possible that the peons sold for pennies objects which are actually very valuable. The Americans in their turn bought what they thought were oddities, never dreaming that they were buying works of art which belong in the museums.

How many of these works of art have survived at all is unknown. Some of them of course have been damaged. In the many revolutions which have rocked the southern nations numerous works of art were used as parts of tents, or the paintings were placed so that they gave shade to the tired soldiers. Some of the art was ruthlessly destroyed by soldiers in their revolutionary desire for destruction. Some was simply thrown away by revolutionaries who wanted something new and who looked down upon the primitive art of their own country. Many times some fine art was thrown on the junk heap while paintings and statues of far less beauty and merit were put in its place.

Sometimes they were simply put away, out of sight, because they were misunderstood and not appreciated properly. Some of them might still be found in the dark corners of Latin America, where they have lain waiting for someone who knows their value to claim them.

What is the value of these items? Whatever the market will bear —depending upon the object's condition, the workmanship and the desire of the buyer.

Where to find them? In all of the countries to the south which knew the influence of the Church. Mexico is especially considered to be one of the finest hunting grounds for the art of these primitive artisans.

Perhaps the bulto or retablo or crucifix which you picked up on your vacation in Mexico might be one that satisfies the demands of the collectors in terms of beauty, workmanship, and age. So many of these primitive works of art have disappeared that your chances for finding one of them are very good.

XVII

AFTER THE PAPER WAS PUT TO BED

Old, Rare Newspapers

N O newspaper was allowed to operate without a license—or to say much of anything against the public officials. Yet early one morning their appeared on the streets of the city the first edition of a newspaper which dared, in spite of all opposition, to speak the truth!

Only four pages long, it told of things which were ordinarily only whispered about on the street corners. It spoke of the savage way in which prisoners were treated by the allies of the editor's own countrymen. Yet it also charged the King of the enemy with immorality. Truth with a vengeance!

Today this sort of reporting would be accepted as a part of a journalist's trade, but at that time it simply was not done. For the year was 1690—and the city was Boston.

The editor was Benjamin Harris, an Englishman, who wrote of the way the Mohawks, England's allies, had savagely treated their French prisoners—and in the next news item spoke of the King of France as being immoral.

This, perhaps, was good reporting, but certainly not good politics, for it took only four days for the colonial authorities to put a stop to it (on the grounds that the little paper had no license)—a stop so effective that for fourteen years no further attempts were made to produce a real American newspaper.

Today, from this one and only issue of the newspaper which Harris called *Publick Occurrences Both Foreign And Domestick,* only one known copy has survived. Sadly enough, this one copy of the first American newspaper is not preserved in America at all, but is filed away in a section called "State Papers Colonial: America and the West Indies" of the Public Records Office in London, England.

Other than this one copy—and a host of reproductions—no other has survived—unless, of course, you can find one. Certainly it should be found, for a copy of the first American newspaper should be on American soil—as well as in the Public Records Office in London, England.

America does, however, possess copies of the first edition of the newspaper which was issued fourteen years after the colonial authorities successfully put a stop to *Publick Occurrences.*

This second, and sometimes called the first "real," newspaper in America was the *Boston News Letter,* which was issued in Boston for many years; but it is the first edition, published in April, 1704, that we are primarily interested in.

There are three copies of this first edition which are known to be extant—and on American ground. One is with the New-York Historical Society in New York; one is with the Massachusetts Historical Society in Boston; and the third is with the American Antiquarian Society in Worcester, Mass.

If there are other extant copies of this first edition of the *Boston News Letter,* they will be in your attic or in your cellar or in the neighborhood second-hand store—waiting for you to find them.

Both of these above lost newspapers are important historically— and this makes them lost treasure—but most of the time copies of old newspapers are worthless unless they are the first printings of a city, county or state, and then there are collectors who want them.

One of these "firsts" is a type of newspaper called the "corantos," the earliest known newspapers printed in the English language, some of them dating back to the early sixteen hundreds. These corantos fall into the lost-treasure class. They are very rare and quite valuable.

Two of the earliest corantos extant are today in the Library of Congress. One of them is dated August 6, 1621; the other is dated October 11 of that same year.

If you could find another copy as early as these, you would have made a real find in the field of lost treasure. Any early newspaper, of course, is at least worth an investigation.

Even before the days of Christ there were such things as "newspapers." The Romans even had journals, and a lot of it was army news, the most important news in the Roman Empire. Some journals, however, told of such items as deaths, punishments, and sacrifices.

Other Roman journals told of the doings of the Senate, and some of the later journals had also accounts of the royal family as well as news of the Senate. Scribes, called Actuarii, took down the speeches of the Senate for publication. In all probability they were the forerunners of our modern-day reporters.

On the other side of the world and at a later date, the oldest daily journal in the world was started. This was the *Peking Gazette,* also known as *Li Chau.* The *Peking Gazette* was first published, believe it or not, in 1340 A.D.

The *Peking Gazette* is still in existence and is an official journal, forming a pamphlet of twenty to forty pages of coarse paper, printed from wooden types on one side only and having a colored paper cover.

Elsewhere—in Venice—the monthly published *Notizie Scritte,* started in 1562, is said to have been the first Italian newspaper. The war which Venice waged in Dalmatia gave rise in 1563 to the custom of having military and commercial information read at a particular place by those desirous of learning the news. A file of these Venetian papers, covering a period of sixty years, is still preserved in the Magliabecchi Library at Florence—extant treasures of another age.

From anywhere in the world and from almost any century, an old newspaper can be treasure—if you can find it and if you recognize it for what it is.

XVIII

The Children's Hour

Childhood Treasures

IN the search for lost treasures of all kinds, not even such a mundane item as the "potty chair" should be overlooked. Potty chairs of the early 1700's actually belong in the museums—and not in your attic or basement.

Shaped like miniature wing chairs with a hole cut in the seat, they may differ a little in design from our modern potty chairs but certainly no one can mistake them for anything else but what they are.

Even potty chairs from a later period, the early 1800's, are worth rescuing from the junk pile, since they can be valued at around $50 apiece, making them worth what little trouble it takes to cart them down from the attic.

Anything the young ones of long ago needed is worth locating. Like the objects made for infants who reached the crawling stage, for among these are the early Colonial "fenders," which were built to keep the little ones from burning themselves in the fireplace.

Or the ladder-back high chairs of the late 1700's. One of these is today on display in Pilgrim Hall, Plymouth, Mass., and if you are lucky enough, you might find another similar to it.

Children's cradles from the Colonial period are items eagerly sought by collectors. Condition and age, of course, are important here, but it is still possible to find them occasionally.

Even the old-fashioned "baby tenders" dating from the 1700's are collectors' items. These were standing stools made complete with a tray for the child's toys.

And then, of course, there are always the "hornbooks!" When America was young, times were very different. Paper was scarce and education was limited. Yet one thing, however, was then as it is today: the general contrariness and destructiveness of the younger generation.

Still, the young ones had to be taught, so the older generation made use of an "elementary school book." This was a "book" which had been used previously in older countries and which is generally called a "hornbook."

The American hornbook consisted of one sheet, on which was printed the alphabet and the Lord's Prayer. To save the sheet, which was considered very precious, it was pasted upon wood and then covered with a thin, transparent piece of horn; thus the name hornbook.

Occasionally there were other items on the page besides the alphabet and the Prayer. There were Roman numerals, capital letters or syllables, and sometimes arithmetic and religious instructions. The page always listed the alphabet in one form or another, and for this reason gained another name: the "abcderia."

Thousands of these abcderias were made in America, yet only very few have ever been located. This is one reason why they are considered collectors' items.

They are also important to us because from them our first Americans learned their daily lessons. However, much to the chagrin of these boys and girls of another day, the hornbook could and was put to an entirely different purpose. The hornbooks were made in the shape of paddles and when the young student did not learn his lesson properly, he was upended and his hornbook used to impress him with the necessity for doing better on the following day.

It must have seemed incongruous to the young student that his hornbook was considered so valuable that he was not allowed to touch it even while studying, but his elders could, and did, use it, of all things, as a paddle.

Of course, not every children's item which you should watch for were so disliked by them. Toys headed the children's list of enjoyable items—and they should be at the top of the treasure hunter's list of odds and ends he might find anywhere, from his attic to his cellar.

Like the toy fire engines made during the 1800's which are now valued at close to $100 apiece. Or toy strollers, the old fashioned wicker kind which you see occasionally at auctions, and which may be valued at $25 or $30, depending on age and condition.

Also, do not forget the trading cards, which were originally put out as part of an advertising scheme. These were the advertisers' commercials of the gay nineties. They were comical or had colorful puzzles on them, or sometimes even pretty girls—all with the purpose of selling something to the consumer.

The children collected them then, as now they collect airplane and baseball cards. Today, these trading cards of yesteryear belong in the hands of the collectors. Value of these cards depends of course on their rarity and condition, but, if you can find a rare example in fine condition, the collectors will buy it eagerly.

Early Colonial or early American toys of any kind are all worth something. It has not been a hundred years since the manufacture of toys became widespread in America. Early toys were made without the benefits of mass production, and because of this they were expensive. Because of this they are also extremely rare and valuable —if you can find them.

This scarcity of toys is not only true of early Colonial toys. It is also true of all the ages before this time, and this is a fact which you must remember when watching for toys.

Toys in Early America were scarce—and dear to the children. Some of the toys were quite old and may even have been brought from Europe by the first pioneers, perhaps even drawn across country in the covered wagons.

Who knows, for instance, in what backwoods second-hand store you might find toys dating back to the times of the Middle Ages! These European toys were often of the finest quality, some of them having been made by the same master goldsmiths who made jewelry and ornaments for the finest gentry. Little toy knights and toy flags with which the children played "crusader."

Sometimes an item from an earlier period than our own might, to our eyes, resemble toys—and yet not have been used as toys at all! Like the fashion dolls which members of European royal families sent to each other, and the Parisian fashion dolls which were set up on display in Europe. Dressed in the rich, luxurious clothing of their times, these fashion dolls of the Middle Ages are today collectors' items. Two dolls of this type are today on display at the University of Upsala in Sweden.

Even in a later period, fashion dolls made to display fashions of the period were popular. Colonial fashion dolls are also collectors' items. Some of them were brought to this country directly from France during the pre-Revolutionary days.

Yet in Colonial days fashion was not the only thing in the minds of the mothers, and dolls were also for the children to play with. Watch for any doll that is this old. You should even investigate hand-whittled wooden dolls for their possible value, as well as any of the cornhusk dolls you might find. These were crude, simple creations made from cornhusks by both the pioneers and the Indians.

There was not even one doll factory in the United States until the late 1800's; dolls were either imported or made by friends or parents. Any of these dolls is worth investigating. German dolls were imported to America for many, many years. These lovely old dolls came all the way from Germany to gladden the hearts of American children. Some had blue eyes, and they are the rarest—and the ones that should be watched for.

Also look for dolls which were made of a combination of wood and pewter. These can be valued at around $80 apiece, if they are old enough, in fine enough condition—and if you can find them.

Also watch for old dolls with china heads. They, too, have become collector's items. Watch for costume dolls. Some of these are quite rare and unusual, and certainly well worth investigating if they are old enough.

Also watch for doll houses, some of which are very old and quite fabulous and, as such, are collectors' items. Complete with dolls, rugs and everything else a real home would have, they belong in the museums—if you can find them. Some of the European doll houses were not made for the children, however, but for the adults. They were large doll houses, sometimes eight feet high, and a few are today in museums in Europe—where you could place another if you could find it.

Most of the doll houses, however, were made for the children, as were the toys, furniture and dolls, but whatever it is, if it belonged to a child and if it is rare enough, old enough and in fine enough condition, the collectors will pay you well for it—if you can find it.

ALL parents who want their children to save money buy banks for them. Or at least that is the way it used to be. Today, it is the parents who want the old banks because they can be lost treasures in disguise.

There are mechanical, semi-mechanical and still banks—all of them worth at least something. Some of them are worth a great deal, depending upon rarity, condition, and age.

There is, of course, no way of telling exactly which banks are missing. What we do have is a series of values for known banks that have passed into or through the hands of the experts—and if you are lucky, you will find similar ones. Or possibly you might even find a very rare bank that has never even been listed.

Values for some of the more valuable known mechanical, semi-mechanical and still banks are as follows:

Afghanistan—$300-$400.
"American Bank" sewing machine—$400.
Aunt Dinah and The Good Fairy—$450.

Billy Goat—$350-$450.
Bowling Alley—$550.
Bread Winners Bank—$350-$400.
Building, Cupola and Man—$400.
Bull and Bear—$200-$600.
Bull—[Charges, tosses boy into well, made of brass] $450-$850.

Called Out—$400-$850.
Camera—$500-$1,000.
Cannon—[Shooting into octagonal fort] $300-$500.
Cat—[Jumps for mouse] $400.
Circus—$600-$1,000.
Confectionary—$450-$700.

Ferris Wheel—$450.
Fort—[Octagonal] $400.
Fortune Teller—["Drop a coin and I will tell your fortune"] $500.
Fortune Teller—[Safe] $400.
Fowler—$450-$650.
Freedman's Bank—[Wood, cloth and white metal, metal clockwork] $650.

Giant—$300-$900.
Girl in Victorian Chair—$325-$750.
Girl Skipping Rope—$550-$800.

Goat, Frog and Old Man—$400-$500.
Grenadier—$200.

Help the Blind—$500.

Initiating—$350-$850.

Katzenjammer—$275-$500.

Locomotive—[Fireman shovels coin into firebox] $500.

Man—[In frock coat, behind grill] $400.
Mikado—$600-$1500.
Motor Bank—$450.

North Pole—$500-$900.
Novelty—["Johnson's Patent"] $400.

Old Woman Who Lived in a Shoe—$600.

Panorama—$300-$400.
Patronize the Blind Man—$400.
Perfection Registering Bank—$500.
Picture Gallery—$200-$500.
Preacher in Pulpit—$400.
Presto—[Mouse comes out of roof] $450.

Ram—[Bucking, boy thumbs nose] $350-$500.
Red Riding Hood—$600.

Shoot the Chute—$500-$1200.

Teddy and The Bear—$75.
Turtle—$400.

Uncle Remus—$450-$600.

Wishbone—$500.
Woman in Shoe—$600.
Woodpecker—[Tree trunk, musical, foreign] $400.

Watch for any of the above. That old bank made to save pennies might turn out to be worth many dollars.

❧

XIX

Money, Money Everywhere

Nickels, Half-Dollars and Dollars

EVERY day you see at least one buffalo nickel—and use it to buy a nickel's worth of gum or pencils or candy. But you ought to look at it more carefully before you spend it, because if it happens to be a 1937 buffalo nickel issued by the Denver mint, *and* if the buffalo has only three legs, then the nickel is worth as much as $125.

So recent yet so valuable—in direct opposition to the popular conception of the value of coins. And one of the most costly mistakes a person looking for rare coins can make is to think that age is a primary factor in determining value.

Coins of ancient Rome, for example, are sometimes worth as little as fifty cents, and some recent coins, such as the above nickel, are worth small fortunes.

Other factors, also, determine the value of a coin. To be valuable a coin must be in excellent condition and be considered a rarity by the collectors. Sometimes a coin is rare because only a few are issued, such as the 1861 Confederate silver half-dollar. Only four of this type and this date were issued, and for this reason the value of this coin can go as high as $20,000. (This is not the restrike of 1879, which is only worth about $200 to $400.)

There are times when a coin is such a rarity that the collectors will pay almost any price for it. One of these is the 1804 silver dollar, so rare that collectors all over the world would bid for it—if you could find it.

Today a few examples of this rare coin have been found and placed in the hands of the collectors. Estimates of this fabled dollar have reached as high as $30,000, a three million percent profit from an investment of a dollar—if you can find one.

Not quite so profitable, yet still high on the treasure hunter's list is an "eight bit" piece which is valued as high as $15,000. This is the Brasher Doubloon, a coin struck in 1787 by Ephraim Brasher.

The Brasher Doubloon is made of gold. On one side of the coin is a mountain with a sun rising behind it, and on the other side is a spread eagle. The coin may also be identified by the punch mark, which is EB.

The Brasher Doubloon, of course, is one of those coins which for most of us automatically suggests great value. This certainly is true but, fortunately for the treasure hunter, there are other coins which should not be overlooked by the seeker of treasures.

One of these is the unc. 1914 D Lincoln cent, either one by one or by the roll. Each of these pennies—if their condition satisfies the numismatists, can be valued as high as $350. A roll of these pennies is worth up to $17,500.

Later in issue, yet still valuable, are the 1921 S Lincoln pennies, which are worth up to $125 apiece—or $6,250 for a roll of fifty.

Many coins are of some value yet not worth fortunes, such as the Massachusetts Pine, Oak, and Willow Tree coins, which are only worth from $50 to $100, or the Sommer Island Shilling, which is valued from $75 to $250. Yet I do not suppose that anyone would willingly throw away coins worth such "minor" value. Even a small return is better than none.

Markets for coins are relatively easy to find. Coin collecting is one of the most common hobbies in the world, and collectors bid eagerly for good specimens. In America alone there are over twenty-five thousand numismatists and well over 100,000 active, enthusiastic "coin collectors." There are coin shops in almost every city, every town, every village in the nation.

Finds have been made in the past and will, undoubtedly, be made again. It is far better to laboriously watch over every coin you receive than to acquire a coin worth a fortune and lose it by handing it out as change to the man at the corner gas station.

Most coin companies will mail their catalogues to you for a nominal price or sometimes for nothing. It is, then, a simple matter to check the coins you have against the coins in the catalogue.

If you should have a coin which you feel is of value, after checking it against a catalogue, do not send it to a dealer. Coins get lost in the mail and it is impossible to insure a coin properly unless you are certain of its value. Also, if the coin is not of value, time and mailing costs have been lost both on your part and on the part of the dealer.

It is far better to make a rubbing of the coin by placing it under a sheet of paper and rubbing gently across it with the edge of a pencil. Do this to both sides of the coin, and then forward the sheet of paper, *not* the coin, to the dealer. If he is interested and it is a rare coin, chances are good that he will reply by return mail.

Also, there are coin clubs in almost every area of the United States, and each member is interested in your coins. If they cannot afford to buy, they at least may tell you who can.

Any coin is worth checking—because it might be worth a fortune. What a shame it would be to spend a $100 nickel on five cent's worth of bubblegum.

XX

THE WALLS ARE EMPTY,
THE FLOORS ARE BARE

Tapestries, Screens, Mirrors and Rugs

IN the Year 1728 in the cathedral of Bayeux a treasure find was made which will be remembered for all time by the lovers of fine and beautiful things. For it was here that the lost Bayeux Tapestry was discovered after having been lost for centuries.

This tapestry is today the most famous of all the extant tapestries in the world; yet it is only twenty inches high. Despite this, however, it has great length, being two hundred and thirty feet long.

Dating from the early Middle Ages, it contains over one thousand figures representing the Norman invasion of England. What a find this was! But there is no way of telling how many other tapestries of enough importance to be classed with the Bayeux are hidden in the other cathedrals and out-of-the-way spots of Europe. Or even how many important or valuable tapestries were brought to America! Brought over to beautify some village church—and then forgotten in the vicissitudes of time. Or ordered sent to them by the suddenly rich gold miners of '49, only to be pawned or lost when the gold gave out.

Today, there are so many types of tapestries which the treasure hunter should watch for that the list is endless.

The Saracens are said to have been making tapestries in France

COLOR PLATES

II to VI

I. "Orange Tree Egg" and "Jeweled 1894 Easter Egg" by Fabergé. (See page 6 or full description.)

III. The "Hercules" is a superb example of a ship's figurehead. It was the first figurehead placed on the bow of the U.S. Frigate "Constitution." *(Ch. X)*

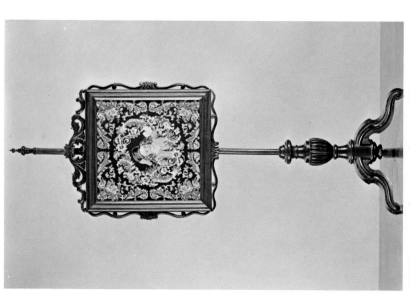

IV. Two magnificent wood-mounted firescreens of the 1860's. At left is a needlepoint screen; a beautiful petit-point screen is at right. (*Ch. XX*)

Courtesy of The Museum of the City of New York

V. This eight-foot-tall grandfather clock was made in 1760 by the Englishman, Charles Howard, of Bristol. *(Ch. XXV)*

VI. Duncan Phyfe made this handsome side table with drawers. The portrait of Henry Post, Jr., was painted by Rembrandt Peale. *(Ch. XXVI)*

as early as the sixth century, but, if they did, there is no evidence to support it. What a triumph for the treasure hunter to find even a fragment of one of these Saracen tapestries, of which, today, there are no known extant examples.

There were the Gothic tapestries of the Middle Ages, and the tapestries of the Renaissance. There were also old German, Italian and Spanish tapestries. Any of these could be valuable if they are rare enough and beautiful enough.

Designs on these old tapestries are often most unusual, such as on one very old extant French tapestry which features that fabulous, non-existent animal, the unicorn. This tapestry hangs today in The Cloisters, in New York City, a part of the Metropolitan Museum's collection.

Aubusson tapestry making goes far back into history. The date at which they were first made is obscure, though certainly it was before the time of Henry IV (1553-1610), who permitted Aubusson works to be brought into the city of Paris duty free. Another tapestry-making house of the seventeenth century was the Gobelin manufactory at Paris.

There were also Japanese tapestries. These were of a very delicate design—and they are very rare. Today, only a very few are in the hands of the collectors, but perhaps you might be the one to find another.

In later European tapestries (approximately after the early 1500's) there were marks on each piece indicating who made them or their town of manufacture. This, however, did not always apply to the smaller pieces, but only to those of larger size. Marks consisted of initials, shields, flowers, towers, etc., and it is a good idea to check for marks on any old tapestry—for they are a good means of authenticating and dating it. Perhaps, if you are lucky enough, you will find one of these fabled, fabulous masterpieces of an almost forgotten art.

TAPESTRIES, however, were not the only objects hanging against the walls of stately homes in the days of yesterday. Then, as now, screens were used to hide corners or portions of rooms, and some of these screens are extant today.

The value of a screen depends, as always, on age, beauty and condition, but screens from any of the past centuries are of value if they can pass the tests of museum curators and antique dealers.

Like one screen of the late 1700's, the Louis XV period, which was evaluated at almost $1,000. Watch for screens of this period—or any of the periods of the past when screens were in use—for, if you are lucky enough, they might be fine enough, old enough and rare enough to equal the value of any screen which is known to be extant today.

Or you might find one of the mirrors which decorated the walls of the wealthy and the rich. Some of these mirrors are so excellent they can be classed with the finest antique furniture on the market. Some of them were imported from England and the rest of Europe—and transported to the United States. Fabulous mirrors that today belong in the museums—if you can find them.

All kinds of mirrors were made—and there are all kinds of mirrors for you to watch for! Among them the mirrors from the Louis XV period, some of them being worth hundreds of dollars. One was recently evaluated at over $600.

Mirrors from any period, if they were associated with the names or styles of the famous furniture makers, are all worth watching for. Some of these mirrors are extant and have had evaluations placed on them. One Chippendale mirror of the 1700's was evaluated at $1,000. Another, an American Chippendale, of the same general period, was evaluated at $1,500.

Watch for any early American mirror—whether of European make and imported, or whether of home manufacture. Most of the early Americans either brought their mirrors with them or sent for them after they were established here.

MANY years ago two Persians offered for sale two old Oriental rugs in bad condition to a rug merchant in Persia. He paid £500 for the pair. One of them he later sold to the Victoria and Albert Museum in London for £2,500. The other one he sold to an American art firm for $57,000!

The rugs were made in the sixteenth century—very old and very lovely. They were museum pieces, but there are today, believe it or not, rugs hidden away in the attics and cellars of American homes which might be priceless—if they were evaluated.

Not all old rugs, of course, have great value, but they are all worth something if they can meet the museum curator's tests for workmanship, age, condition and beauty.

Any old rug is worth an evaluation. Any rug which is old enough and has the nomenclature of "oriental," has fine detail and exquisite workmanship, and can pass the test for rarity, is of value to the finder. Any rug which looks Oriental is worth an examination by an expert.

Some of these rugs are today almost forgotten—the Kulahs, the Sennas, the Derbends and the Daghestans. But *you* should never forget them—there might be one in your attic.

One of the most famous makes of all the Oriental carpets was the Isfahan (Ispahan). It was noteworthy especially for the beauty of its varying shades of red (although carpets may be Isfahans without being red, this being merely their favorite and probably most beautifully worked color). A mere fragment of a sixteenth-century Ispahan carpet has been valued at $6,000.

The Ladik rugs are also considered among the finest Oriental carpets in the world, yet they were, at one time, considered almost valueless. But in recent years the beauty and rarity of this rug have been realized and so today the value spirals upwards.

The Persians made rugs so delicately worked that there would be hundreds of knots per square foot of carpeting. The quality of a Persian carpet may be illustrated by the fact that there are in Persia today rugs still in use which were made in the late 1500's.

There was also a type of rug made first in Kerman and later at a place near Ispahan. These latter carpets are so lovely in beauty and in texture that, although they were made of wool, only the most astute testing will prove them not to be silk. There were fine rugs made at Bergama also, the most famous being certain small rugs with a medallion in the center.

We always think of the Oriental carpet as being a thing of delicate and almost miniature detail. But originally the rugs of the tribes were composed of designs which were both brilliant in hue and great in size, so that a traveler or fellow nomad could distinguish the tribal tents from a great distance. Thus, each design came to represent a certain tribe, and each traveler knew his friend or enemy by the color and design of his tent—which he could ascertain from a safe and lengthy distance.

The Chinese made rugs which they wrapped around the pillars supporting the roofs of their temples. Many times real gold was used in these rugs.

There also were, and are, prayer rugs, and they are possibly among the most beautiful rugs ever made. A prayer rug, usually the size of a small throw rug, can be recognized by the mihrab design, which looks like a niche or an altar. The niche, or mihrab, of the Mohammedan prayer rug is always pointed toward Mecca, the worshipper then kneeling upon this carpet, which is usually his finest rug, pertaining to his religious and not to his daily life.

There was a period during the Middle Ages when only the noble-born could own a rug. These rugs were spread before the thrones of the great, and to be called "on the carpet" was often a frightening experience for anyone appearing before his lord. Today, "common" people own rugs and floor coverings, yet the expression to be "on the carpet" retains its rather grim meaning.

Also in the Middle Ages, the wealthy covered their tables with rugs, and they canopied the statues of their favorite saints with fine carpets, and sometimes the rug would be placed on the floor before the altar in a church. Also a typical use for rugs during that period was their draping over balconies on great fete days and during coronation processions.

In the same period the Spaniards, who intermarried into the English court, did many things which their English hosts neither understood nor appreciated. Such was the case of one Spanish princess who shocked the English by placing rugs on the floors of her rooms and then, wonder of wonders, she actually walked on them.

It was also during this era that France made her own carpets as well as importing what she could. These French rugs were called "Saracen carpets." By royal order of the King of France, a carpet factory was started in 1604 where the Savonnerie carpets were made. Early carpets were also made in Spain and in Venice.

Yet the rugs which were made in Europe were not the "true" Oriental rugs. They retained the flavor of the Orient, but did not follow the traditional Oriental pattern.

And later, by the middle of the eighteenth century, England also had its place for making carpets—the town of Exeter. America had her carpets, too, and these also are of some worth to the treasure hunter, although of very little value compared to the older and finer rugs of an earlier date.

We know definitely that carpets were imported and sold here by the 1760's, but it was not until the 1790's that a "carpet factory" appeared in America. Yet, whether the rugs you find are American,

English or Oriental, if you can find any of the older carpets and they can pass the rigid tests of the experts who know fine and rare carpets, then you, truly, have found treasures underfoot.

XXI

BOOK MADNESS

Rare and Valuable Editions

COLLECTORS and buyers of rare books often become so avid in their desire for books that there is even a special name for their "hobby": bibliomania, a name taken from the Greek, meaning book-madness.

Bibliomaniacs are willing to go to almost any length to find and purchase copies of books which they deem rare, and they do not stop at books of one particular nation or author.

There is one author, however, whose works they desire above all others. His name is known to every schoolboy in every school in almost every nation of the world: William Shakespeare.

The Pavier Quarto edition of the plays of Shakespeare is both rare and valuable. It is so rare that the copy of this edition which is in the Folger Shakespeare Library in Washington, D.C., is probably the only one extant today—unless, of course, you can find another one.

To remember to watch for Shakespeare's plays is simple. But there are other missing works whose worth—or even how many of them are missing—is unknown. Like the works of Sir Walter Raleigh.

These are poems which were praised highly during his lifetime, yet most of his poetry was never even published and, today, a great many of his poems may have been lost to us forever—unless you can find them. Their value would, of course, depend on which ones they were and how eagerly the collectors would bid for them.

They could be anywhere! Books and manuscripts have been found in the strangest places—even in the Leningrad Archives, which announced recently that they had found manuscripts and letters by such famous authors as James Fenimore Cooper, Hans Christian Andersen and Sir Walter Scott.

The value of these manuscripts and letters would, naturally, depend upon what condition they were in, and condition means very much when placing a value on a book. One very good example of this would be the *Pickwick Papers,* by Dickens. There are two editions of this book, but their difference in value because of difference in condition makes one edition merely a "nice find" and the other a found treasure.

The edition of *Pickwick Papers* which is merely a nice find is the one which was a rebound issue of the original. This rebound volume (without wrappers) is worth only about $25 to $50. A nice find. But the other issue is the original, the one which was to be later rebound. The original edition was, of course, in different form. It was issued in separate parts in printed wrappers. And this issue—if you can find a copy of it—is worth between $25,000 and $50,000!

There are other authors' books which are also worth great sums of money. To the bibliomaniac the name of Edgar Allan Poe is a magic name. His work *Tamerlane and Other Poems,* the 1827 edition, is regarded as one of the rarest books in American literature. In the past a copy of it has brought $25,000, and today chances are that the value of another copy would be much higher since none has turned up in recent years.

These are tremendous prices for a book that is covered with a drab-color paper wrapper—yet anything by Poe has magic to it, not only to the treasure hunter but to aspiring writers as well. So efficacious was the name Poe to the public and to the literary critics of at least one generation that one aspiring writer published a poem which he claimed to have been written by Poe. He claimed the poem as a new find in literature—a poem which he said was found at an inn near Richmond, Virginia, written on the flyleaf of a copy of *Ainsworth's Dictionary.*

What a find such a poem would be to any treasure hunter! But in this case, it just was not so. The budding author had written it himself. He called the poem "Leonanie." He was only trying to prove, he said later, that if he wrote under a famous name, his poetry would receive recognition.

He did receive recognition during his lifetime—not because of the poem, however, but rather in spite of it, since the whole thing was nothing but a fraud.

The budding writer's name? James Whitcomb Riley.

Poe's is a magic name—not only to writers but to treasure hunters as well. There are today twelve extant copies of Poe's *Tamerlane*. Any way you look at it, this leaves a remainder of twenty-eight, since there were forty copies printed!

Twenty-eight missing copies of a book that is known to be a treasure of American literature! Dingy books hidden in someone's attic or someone's cellar—waiting for you to find them and turn them into gold.

Don't disregard any old-looking book. There are so many stories about the works of Edgar Allan Poe which only serve to point out the foolishness of not checking into the value of any old book you might have lying around.

There is the story of the old lady who used a first edition of Poe to prop up the leg of an old dresser in the cellar of her home. And there is the story of the first edition of Poe's works which was given away to a junk dealer—because the person who had it did not know what he had.

If you have any old book, it is usually possible to check its edition, title and author against lists of rare books which most librarians can give you. One thing to watch for, of course, is *any* first edition by any author whose name is familiar to you. If the author has become famous since his first book was published and the issue date was years ago, it is more than probable that the book is worth something.

Any old book is worth checking. Your librarian will help you. Your local book dealer will help you. From Shakespeare to Poe, if it is a first edition, chances are that you have made a find in the field of bibliomania, the book madness which seems to strike the book collectors at the sight of a rare book which they decide they must have—and would seemingly pay any price for.

IN the city of London, an auctioneer went through what he thought was just another pile of books. They had been dumped into an old basket and the job was pretty monotonous. The hope of ever really finding a treasure seemed remote. Usually, the stuff found was just junk.

Suddenly his eyes lighted up. For this time the basket was not filled with junk. This time he had come upon a basket of gold—for in the basket was a prayer book, a very old and rare prayer book.

Nervously, he picked it up. It was Flemish—and over five hundred years old. So rare, and so valuable that when it was finally put up for sale, it went for the fabulous sum of $89,000!

This sale almost set a record in the history of book sales. Yet at least one other book brought in a higher price at auction, a price which reached the incredible sum of $150,000.

This sum was paid for a copy of the *Bay Psalm Book* at a sale in the Parke Bernet Auction Galleries in New York. It was one of the highest prices ever received at auction for a printed book—and it is the price you might receive if you could find another copy of the *Bay Psalm Book*.

It was the first book to be printed in the American colonies. Printed in 1640, it was the work of Stephen Daye, but such men as Richard Mather, Thomas Wilde and John Eliot all worked together on it. They, in their efforts to print a psalm book, produced not only a religious book—they produced one of the rarest lost treasures in the field of bibliomania. A copy of this book is a treasure well worth searching for, one you might receive $151,000 for—if you can find it.

Yet even this fabled price is not the most a book can be worth. There are missing copies of another religious book which are worth approximately a third of a million dollars apiece if you can find one of them. And strangely enough, this is a lost treasure that most everyone believes does not exist.

Because the book is so well known, it is felt that if there were any of them still around, they would have been found long ago. But this is not true. There were approximately two hundred copies of this book printed—yet there are only forty-six copies that have been found! The question is: what happened to the other one hundred and fifty-four copies?

One hundred and fifty-four copies of a book simply do not disappear. Some of them, of course, will be damaged or destroyed but not all one hundred and fifty-four.

Where are they—these one hundred and fifty-four copies of the fabled, the fabulous, the magnificent *Gutenberg Bible*? Frederick R. Goff, Chief, Rare Book Division, Library of Congress, has chosen the *Gutenberg Bible* as one of the most valuable books in the world. It was the first printed book in Europe, having been printed in the early fifteenth century at Mainz, Germany. Rare and valuable, this is, surely, a treasure hunter's dream. There are only three perfect copies of the great *Gutenberg Bible* known to be in existence— and the Library of Congress has one of these. You might have another copy and not even know it. Look again at that old bible in the attic. It just might be worth a third of a million dollars!

Value of a *Gutenberg Bible*, of course, would depend upon its condition. This is true of any rare book. Yet a copy of this great Bible could be worth a third of a million, if it were in the same fine condition as the copy in the Library of Congress which was purchased from Dr. Otto Vollbehr, who originally paid approximately a third of a million for it. Today the Library considers this copy as being "almost priceless."

Remember, of course, that the price of a rare book goes up and up as time goes by. The value of the *Gutenberg Bible* has gone up from $25,000 to $50,000, to $106,000, to $120,000, to a third of a million dollars—and the price is still going up.

Any book printed by Gutenberg is of value today if it is in fine condition. But Gutenberg in his lifetime did not always do so well. He failed, just at the time when printing was getting started. He had borrowed money from the money lender Johann Fust, and, when Gutenberg failed, Fust stepped in and took his equipment to make up for the mortgage which Gutenberg could not pay off.

The main item Fust took, in terms of bibliophilic history, was the printing press. But he did not let the printing press lie idle. With his son-in-law Peter Schöffer he continued to print, and one of the books which Fust and Schöffer printed was the *Psalter of 1457*, a book which, in value, stands second only to Gutenberg's Bible.

No copy of the *Psalter of 1457* is owned by any American library. It is this rare. Technically a book of psalms, it contains three hundred and fifty pages. The initials in the book are printed in red and blue. It was the first printed book which had a *complete* date in it. It was also the first printed book to have a colophon (the printer's name and the place at which the book was printed).

It is a rarity well worth your time and trouble. Remember, the last quoted price for the great *Gutenberg Bible* was a third of a million dollars—and the *Psalter of 1457* stands second to it. Remember this the next time you run across an old book of psalms! It just might be the right edition!

Sometimes, of course, it is much harder to put a price on a missing book, but often the history behind the book makes even the very printing of it an extraordinary thing—as the book printed in America at the direct order of a man who called himself a king.

Though there is no king in the United States, not so long ago a man ruled his subjects by his own laws and called himself by that forbidden title. King of his people and of his territory, he ruled with an iron hand and even coined his own money.

His own people murdered him. They were the Strangites, a branch of the Mormons, and their king was James Jesse Strang, or "King James," according to the way he told it. He claimed to be Joseph Smith's successor, yet originally he had been driven away from the main body of the Mormons because he had disagreed with Brigham Young. He fled to Big Beaver Island in the northern part of Lake Michigan in Charlevoix County in 1847 and settled there with those of his followers who still believed in him. Those who went with him followed his leadership implicitly—until he introduced polygamy in 1849.

This fomented trouble and in 1856 Strang's monarchical bubble burst and he was murdered. The little colony became, then, a thing of the past. Today the most important reminder of their subjugation to their king is a book, *The Book the Law of the Lord.*

It was printed at St. James, the town set up on Big Beaver Island, which King James named after himself. He ordered the printing of this book, which laid down the rules which he stipulated for his people.

Today there are only two copies of this book known to be extant. One is in the Huntington Library. The other is with the firm of Eberstadt in New York.

One possible reason why only two copies are in existence is that, when Strang was murdered, his "kingdom" was ravaged, and probably many copies of the book were destroyed. Yet there is always the chance that there are other copies in existence today—waiting for you to find them.

The value of a copy of this book depends on what the collector will pay and how badly he wants it. Any old book is worth investigating—and if you are lucky enough you might find anything from the *The Book the Law of the Lord* to another copy of the great *Gutenberg Bible*.

WHEN the bibliomaniacs reach out their hands for rare books, there is no limit to the country, the language or the contents of the work which they desire to own.

Among the many items which they desire is a pamphlet with the long title of the *Short Ravelings From a Long Yarn, Or Tales Of The Santa Fe Trail,* published in 1847. The value of this pamphlet has been quoted at up to one thousand dollars, and today there are only four copies of it known to exist. However, there might be another one stuck away in your bookcase or in that old box of junk you have been meaning to throw away—if you take the time and trouble to look through it.

Another book collectors would gladly buy from you is the *History of New York* by Washington Irving. Supposedly written by an eccentric Dutchman, Diedrich Knickerbocker, the book is considered to be a masterpiece of satire. Published in 1809, it is referred to as "Knickerbocker's History of New York from the Beginning of the World to the End of the Dutch Dynasty." It is a collector's item, a book for which they will pay you varying prices depending upon the condition of the copy which, if you are lucky enough, you will find.

A copy in poor condition might bring you $50. A better copy might bring you $125. An even better copy might fetch $150. But an unbattered copy, in the same fine condition as when it left the hands of the printer, could bring you $1,000 if you are lucky enough to find one.

Any old book in fine condition is worth being evaluated by an expert. Even schoolbooks have been known to have value. In early America there were generations of children who learned their ABC's by reciting "In Adam's Fall, We Sinned All;" B's were "The Life to Mend, This Book Attend," and facetious C was learned as "The Cat doth Play and after slay."

These, together with the remainder of the alphabet, illustrated by crude wood-cuts, comprised a portion of the first important textbook in America. In opposition to the hornbook, which it supplanted, the *New England Primer* possessed leaves and binding. It contained, besides the alphabet, the Ten Commandments, religious verses, spelling words, and the catechism.

Although the original author of this book is unknown, it was compiled by Benjamin Harris, a Boston printer. It was an abridgment of an earlier work, *The Protestant Tutor,* and as an educational force it was tremendously influential in the lives of many generations of young Americans. There were at least forty editions of the *New England Primer,* the first printed in 1690, yet there are only a very few extant today—and hardly any of the first edition.

For over a hundred years the children of America studied from this book, yet so very few have survived. One of these, the "Bradford Fragment," was located in the binding of a later book.

Out of forty editions, surely somebody's 'attic bookcase holds a copy. Even a badly mutilated copy could have some value. In 1926 one very bad copy, dated 1768, sold for $150. With luck the treasure hunter might locate a copy dated in the 1690's—and it might even be in good condition. It might, even today, be hidden away in your cellar, your attic, or anywhere, if you just take the time and trouble to check.

One individual apparently forgot this prime rule of treasure hunting, because he did not check. And because he did not check he gave away a book that was worth $250. Certainly too valuable a work to give away! The book, a first-edition pamphlet of *A Boy's Will,* by Robert Frost, was discovered by librarians at Marquette University as they searched through a box of books which had been donated to the school.

Probably no one will ever know how many rare books have been destroyed or thrown away because the owners did not know what they had. Even the bindings on a book can have value—but do not tear away the bindings in your attempt to sell them. Leave them intact, for only in fine condition do they have value. Watch for the bindings of Zaehnsdorf, Hayday, Charles Lewis, Derome, Rivière, Roger Payne, Padeloup, Bedford and Bozerian.

Bindings, books, or manuscripts—there are works from every nation and every century worth watching for. There are works upon which no value can be placed until they are found. The treasure hunter must first locate them and then present them for sale, hoping for a high bid from the collectors. However, the first thing is to find them.

Sometimes, of course, it is even a problem as to whether or not a work is actually missing—like the original of *The Kings of Britain*. The *Historia de Gestis Regum Brittanniae* (The History of the Kings of Britain) contained a supposed genealogy of the kings of Britain and was written by Geoffrey of Monmouth in the twelfth century. Yet when Geoffrey wrote this history he claimed that he was writing only a translation of an earlier work. It is this earlier work about which is raised the question of whether or not it ever existed. The authorities doubt that it ever existed at all—but what a find for the treasure hunter if it could be located!

There is, however, one work in connection with *The Kings of Britain* which we know is missing. This is a portion of a rhymed French translation of the work, by Geoffrey Gaimar. Today, only approximately a third of this rhymed translation is extant. The other two thirds of the work are lost—waiting for the treasure hunter.

In watching for lost works of the past, the name of the Venerable Bede must not be forgotten, for he was an ardent and prolific writer. He, allegedly, wrote more than forty pieces, and in the year 735, as he lay dying, he was still writing. He was, with his last breath, still pouring out new works, and one of these, a translation of the Gospel of St. John, is now lost.

The man to whom Bede dictated this work, which even the fear of death could not stop, was the man we know as Saint Cuthbert. According to Cuthbert, Bede loved Anglo-Saxon poetry, but whatever Bede may have written in this style there are only two lines we definitely know to have been his—and these are from a poem quoted by Cuthbert.

We know, however, that one of Bede's works, the translation of the New Testament, did exist in manuscript form. Today this translation has disappeared.

There is also another work, a handbook by King Alfred, which did exist as a manuscript but which today is missing. This, too, has disappeared from the world of literature—unless you can find it.

Many early manuscripts are still missing, including early French lais of the pre-twelfth-century period. From the late eleven hundreds there is one which should especially be watched for. It is from the pen of Robert de Boron, one of the more prominent writers of that century.

It was toward the end of this period that he wrote three different manuscripts: *Merlin*; *Joseph*; and *Perceval*. A part of the *Merlin* has been preserved; all of *Joseph* has been preserved; but *Perceval* is missing—unless you can find it.

Books, bindings, and manuscripts, they are worth their weight in gold—if you can find the right ones.

XXII

Rare Illustrations

Works of Dürer, Schöngauer, Mantegna, Sartain, and Others

THE convent library contained many books and manuscripts of all sizes and shapes, and anyone who looked through the large collection could halfway expect to find a rare book or lost manuscript—but this time they found neither a rare book nor an expensive manuscript but rather something which had been pasted to the inside of one of the manuscripts.

It was a lost woodcut, one of the finest in the world. Dated 1423, and therefore one of the first of the woodcuts or engravings to appear in Europe, it represented Saint Christopher, the patron saint of travelers and a popular subject in the days when it was made.

The engravings and woodcuts of that day were often crude and rough, but sometimes they were great works of art, and lucky is the treasure hunter who finds one which fits into this category of fine art.

Most of these early woodcuts, made by impressing inked wood on paper, represented some form of Biblical scene, or episodes from the lives of the saints, but slowly this art form turned away from the Biblical toward the more mundane aspects of the everyday life of the people. Even books began to use pictures as an aid in instruction in reading.

Cologne, Augsburg and Nuremberg were prominent centers for these earlier wood engravings, and examples of this art have been spread and lost throughout the world. One of the earliest and certainly the most famous of the engravers of this period was Albrecht Dürer (1471-1528). He was German, and in his home town of Nuremberg, woodcuts and engravings were a very popular form of art expression.

Dürer created both copper engravings and woodcuts, and he also made book illustrations, coats-of-arms and, during his very early years, line drawings, which he sold to armorers and silversmiths.

If you should find a woodcut or engraving which you think might have been made by Dürer during his younger years, have it checked carefully. During his early years he worked of necessity surrounded by other people, and doubt is cast upon many of the woodcuts and engravings from this period of his life. Some of them are genuine, of course, but some of them are considered to be of questionable authorship.

Dürer did have one way, however, of signing many of his works which is of great help to the treasure hunter in ascertaining their authenticity. This was the Albrecht Dürer monogram, in which the A is comparatively large and straddles a smaller D. Watch for this monogram, because it is important.

One of the most famous examples of the extant work of Dürer is in the *Apocalypse* printed in 1498, only six years after Columbus discovered the new world.

In this work is one woodcut which is especially famous, "The Four Horsemen of the Apocalypse." It was made to illustrate a part of the "Book of Revelations," and in 1498, the year the woodcut was made, Dürer's wife sold copies of it at country fairs. No one knows how many of these copies are missing, but certainly there should be at least a few left in someone's attic or old trunk or pasted in the pages of a book. Nor is there a definite value for these copies. The trick is to find a collector who really wants them.

They certainly are worth a great deal—if you find the right collector. But anything by Dürer is worth watching for, and any of these early woodcuts are worth your time and trouble.

There are also other engravers whose works you should watch for, such as Martin Schöngauer (1445?-1491) and Andrea Mantegna (1431-1506).

These masters, however, are not the only ones, for the arts of woodcutting and engraving moved westward to the new world and also early American woodcuts and engravings are among the items that the treasure hunter should watch for.

Many early American artists were famous in this field: Sartain, who introduced mezzotint to America; Benson John Lossing, who, among other things, did illustrations for the *Family Magazine*; Alexander Anderson, who made the first wood engravings in the United States and whose illustrations included such items as plates for Shakespeare's plays and *Webster's Elementary Spelling Book*. He also did work for Thomas Bewick's *Birds* and for Charles Bell's *Anatomy*.

Also there was Peter Maverick, who made engravings of Dunlap's painting of Benjamin Moore and Charles King's painting of Henry Clay.

Asher Brown Durand was also one of these early American artists whose engravings should be watched for. He created many works, including some which he made by copying prints from books, as well as an engraving of Trumbull's Declaration of Independence.

One other, and probably the most well known of these artists, was Paul Revere, who engraved on copper. The name Revere, if you can find it on an engraving, speaks for itself, for there is nothing that Revere made that does not have value to the collectors.

The name Revere is so well known today that it needs no further explanation. This is also true of the prints by Currier and Ives. There have been so many copies of these prints made that it is doubtful that there is a family in America which does not have, or at least at one time had, a Currier and Ives copy hanging on the wall.

What most people do not realize, however, is that the "originals" of these copies are today very rare. They are also very expensive. There are all kinds of Currier and Ives prints to watch for, because they made so many of them—over four thousand prints signed with their names.

They were prints of almost every phase of American life—snow scenes, holiday scenes, railroads, disasters, ships, etc. Over four thousand of them—enough to make the treasure hunter's chances of finding an original pretty good.

If you should find an old print, etching, engraving, or woodcut, take it to an expert. The value of these items depends on so many variables—the date, the condition, the artistry of the man who made it. All of these variables make the hunt for etchings, engravings, woodcuts, and prints similar to taking a chance in a lottery. Sometimes you make a hit and sometimes you don't—but the chances for a long shot are good—if you look long enough and hard enough, and have just a little bit of luck.

Remember that these works could be anywhere at all, like the Revere engraved copperplate which was found in, of all places, a junk pile all the way across the ocean from where Revere first made it: in Scotland!

XXIII

GOLD DUST IN A BALL OF WAX

Carvings, Cigar-Store Indians,
Hitching Posts, Barbers' Poles

WHEN today's advertising man has a new idea, his confreres eye him skeptically and say, "All right, let's roll it up in a ball of wax and toss it around a little." When yesterday's store owner, who was also his own advertising man, had a new idea, his words on the subject were perhaps not as colorful but he would think it over a little and then hire a carver to make a figure that would be representative of his business.

After weeks of labor, the figure would be ready and would be proudly placed on display outside the door of the shop to let the passersby know the type of goods sold within. And if the figure was skillfully executed it would attract many viewers—and many buyers.

The purpose of advertising certainly has not changed, even though the gimmicks have. These older gimmicks, however, these carved figures of another day, are worth a great deal of money to the modern collector.

Perhaps, in our modern efforts to reach more people, we have neglected fine artistry. Perhaps this is one reason why collectors of today place such a high value on the advertising gimmicks of yesterday, for they are not only antiques but memories of a past which we will never see again.

All sorts of carved figures stood in front of the shops, and they were a familiar sight both in England and in America. Everyone who entered a shop passed one of these gaily painted figures as he went in.

Today their value is tremendous, depending, of course, upon condition, rarity, etc. A carved race track tout was recently appraised at over $2,000. Another shop figure, a captain, was appraised at over $3,000.

If you should find an odd figure, a real rarity, not just the run-of-the-mill cigar-store Indian, the chances are, if it is in good condition, that it is worth a great deal.

Yet even the cigar-store Indian can be worth at least something, depending again on age and condition. These wooden Indians were a symbol of the old-time American tobacco shops. They were a very common sight in the United States.

The cigar-store Indian industry in America was a going business selling approximately three hundred figures yearly, yet today there are only a few left, some of them in museums and collections. But perhaps there are many more around—waiting in your neighborhood lumber yard or even in your attic.

Sometimes these "Indians" are in bad condition, but, if you can find a collector who really wants one, it is possible that he would be willing to buy it first and then rejuvenate it.

In Westchester, California, there is a tobacco shop called Clyde's Pipe Rack, and in the front of the store stands Princess Minnehaha —a one-hundred-year-old wooden beauty, one of the last of America's wooden Indians. Not too long ago, however, Princess Minnehaha was in very sad condition, but the owners of the shop, Mr. and Mrs. Clyde Strawn, scraped away at the layers of old paint until they were down to the original—then carefully they repainted her to her original colors. Today Princess Minnehaha stands once more in front of a tobacco shop, as lovely as she was a hundred years ago.

Certainly if you could find a wooden Indian, it is worth investigating. The collectors are so avid that all members of the "Society for the Preservation of the Wooden Indian" have sworn to ". . . never . . . destroy their Indians and to let the Society know if they ever want to dispose of them, so they can be passed along to other collectors."

Any wooden Indian you may find is worth something, but there are other types of wooden figures, like the "Race Track Tout" and the "Ship Captain," which are worth a great deal of money. They are, however, more rare and harder to find and therefore of much greater value than the more common Indians.

Many of these figures which were not Indians were English, since the British "cigar-store Indians" were not Indians at all but "black boys" and "smoke shop figures."

One smoke shop figure, a sultan, was recently appraised at $525 —certainly worth watching for.

No one knows where all of these figures are today. They were eventually taken off the streets because of sidewalk restrictions. These ordinances killed one of our traditions, by causing the cigar-store Indian to pass into history—and on to the treasure hunter's list.

Not eliminated by these sidewalk restrictions, but fading from the scene simply because the march of progress made them obsolete, were the old-fashioned hitching posts.

They were put up by shop proprietors for their customers' convenience, in much the same way today's store owners provide parking lots for their customers.

Today the hitching post is forgotten—except by the collectors, who will pay as much as $250 for a rare and fine example.

There is one other item, however, which has not been eliminated from the American scene. Neither sidewalk restrictions nor modern progress has caused the barber pole to fade from our streets. But it is the *antique* barber pole which you should watch for; the modern ones, of course, are worth something only to the barbershop owner and not the collector.

The very old barber poles were complete with red pole, a bowl, and a strip of cloth. The red pole represented both the color of blood and the stick which the patient gripped tightly while the barber-surgeon did his job of blood-letting. The bowl would collect the dripping blood. The strip of cloth was used by the barber-surgeon to bandage his patient when he was through.

The barber's pole with the bowl was a rarity in America, but there were many of the more common bowl-less types which are now disappearing from the scene because people who do not realize that they are worth anything either destroy or throw them away.

Even a nineteenth-century barber's pole is worth around $60, and the older ones, of course, are worth much more. Whether you find a wooden shop figure or an old barber's pole, do not throw it away or burn it or repaint it. It may be something a collector would buy in a minute—if you would just give him a chance.

XXIV

GLASS AND MORE GLASS

Venetian to Stiegel

THE world's most valuable example of the glass blower's art is the Portland Vase—a vase which the British Museum refused to sell even when offered fifty thousand dollars for it.

While it is extremely unlikely that the modern treasure hunter would find another Portland vase, still there are other examples of the glass blower's art which the treasure hunter should watch for.

Some of them will be worth only a few dollars, but some of them —if they finish out a set or if they are rare examples—can be worth a great deal.

Probably among the best known of the collectors' items—so rare and so valuable that most of the extant examples are in museums— are the glass objects of the Venetians. Venetian glass, as we know it, was made from the eleventh century until it reached its peak in the seventeenth century. There were, of course, other periods of Venetian glass making, but it is to these centuries that we must look for our museum pieces.

The art of glass making was so well regarded in Venice during this period that laws were passed regarding its manufacture. To protect the secrets of the methods which they used, the Venetians moved their entire glass industry onto the island of Murano, where armed guards walked the streets at night to protect the workers.

The workers themselves were executed if they betrayed the secrets of their profession, but if they were loyal to the industry they became prosperous.

Even exportation of the raw materials from which the glass was made was prohibited. Yet, even with all precautions, other nations sent in agents to try to learn the secret of how the fabled Venetian glass was made. It was not considered enough to merely have patrolling guards as protection against these foreign agents. Professional murderers were hired who eliminated the foreign agents, thereby "protecting" the secrets of the glass which today museums all over the world are anxious to have.

Among the most beautiful of the Venetian glass was the so-called "Cristallo" glass, which was very thin and which was twisted into many shapes. It was clear glass although it had a slight grayishness of color. There is also a type of Venetian glass that is white and clear combined and so finely woven that it is called "Lace Glass."

Yet, valuable as Venetian glass is, it is far more probable that the first thing the glass hunter will find will be American glass. Among these, if the treasure hunter is lucky enough, will be Wistar glass, Sandwich glass and Amelung glass.

Wistar glass is a "must" on the treasure hunter's list. In regard to the actual finding of Wistar glass, John C. Sheppard, Personnel Department, Glassboro Plant, Glassboro, N.J., says, "Whatever . . . (Wistar glass) . . . might be in existence would more than likely be in a museum." This does not, however, preclude the possibility that the treasure hunter might find a new and rare piece.

Caspar Wistar was a German button maker from Philadelphia. He imported glass workers from Belgium in the early 1700's and began his glassworks in a settlement called, appropriately enough, "Wistarberg," which was in the county which is now called Salem in New Jersey.

This Wistar factory was the first important glass factory in America. Window and bottle glass are among the important items to look for that were made in Caspar Wistar's factory. Other objects, such as bowls and household glass, were not made in the factory during working hours, but the workmen made these items for their own personal use to take home with them. They made them, supposedly, after working hours, and these, too, are items to watch for.

Caspar Wistar died in 1752. His son Richard carried on his father's business, until the year 1782. But there was another area where Wistar-type glass was made. The art was perpetuated as "Wistar type" glass by several workmen from Caspar Wistar's factory who also worked for themselves in Glassboro, N. J.

In 1781, according to local records, the Stanger Brothers, all four of them, went to Glassboro and opened a factory of their own. However, this factory failed and they sold it to Heston and Carpenter.

Heston and Carpenter sold out in their turn (shortly after 1800) to Ebenezer Whitney, and for over a hundred years the Whitney family made glass in Glassboro. Then they, too, sold out, this time to the Owens Bottle Company, which is still in operation today.

Thus, for over a hundred and fifteen years, Glassboro, New Jersey has produced glass which it is well for the treasure hunter to watch for, remembering of course that it will be the early pieces of this glass that you want.

Glass, either Wistar or "Wistar type" is well worth the time and effort of the vigilant treasure hunter.

Sandwich glass must also be on the treasure hunters' list. Worth from $10 or $15 apiece, every piece of Sandwich glass is worth something; and some pieces of Sandwich glass, if they are rare enough or finish out a collection, can fetch a great deal.

For example, a decanter of an ordinary Sandwich pattern sells for around $40 and a compote might sell for around $100—but find a piece of Sandwich that is rare or that can finish out a collector's set and you might get many times that amount.

Sandwich is a name familiar to all lovers of glassware and should be familiar to all treasure hunters as well, since collectors in all parts of the world desire rare and fine pieces of this glass.

Starting about 1825, glass was made in Sandwich, Massachusetts, and they continued to make it there for over fifty years by a process which has now been lost.

Until the 1820's glass was all hand blown, but at about this time Deming Jarvis, together with Enoch Robinson, made several machines which pressed glass by a process which made it possible to press glass into an iron mold and then stamp a pattern on it.

The new machines were so successful that old-fashioned glassmakers who were still trying to make a livelihood by hand-blowing glass became enraged at Deming Jarvis, because by using his machines, pressed glass could be produced at only a fraction of the cost of hand-blown glass.

Afraid that they would kill him, Jarvis hid. Yet, even though he had to hide in fear of his life, Jarvis continued working with his new machines. He was the owner of the Sandwich Glass Company, which became very successful.

Jarvis was ahead of his time in many ways. He was vitally interested in the welfare of his workmen, and he helped them to such an extent that they returned his help by enabling the Sandwich Glass Company to withstand even the depressions of the period.

Although pressed glass was made in many places, it was in Sandwich, Mass., that it found its niche in the world of fine glass—and found its way onto the treasure hunter's list.

The third well known type of American glass desired by collectors is Amelung glass, made in the Amelung Glass Factory, which was established near Frederick, Maryland, in the late 1700's. The factory failed, but the examples of their work—if you can find any of them—will be well worth your time. Some of these pieces of glass made in the Amelung factory were probably the only pieces of early American glass which were inscribed and dated.

There are many types of glass worth watching for. The list is almost endless. Patterned glass of any kind can be valuable. Certain pieces, of course, are very rare and therefore more sought after, like the "Bellflower" patterned cake plates which can be worth $250 apiece. Or the "Horn of Plenty" patterned dishes and cake plates which bring as much as $300 if they are of rare size and shape.

"Thumbprint" patterned punch bowls and compotes, in certain sizes, may be valued as high as $400; "Sandwich Star" patterned compotes can be worth $250; "Blackberry" patterned milk-white water pitchers are sometimes valued at a couple of hundred dollars.

All of them, of course, must be the ones that are the rare shapes, sizes, etc.

Also included among the American types to watch for is Amberina glass, a special type of glass into which gold had been put. The colors are amber, yellow and red, and the pieces were made during the nineteenth century in Massachusetts.

Peach Bloom glass, also made in Massachusetts during the same period, is another type to watch for. There are also examples of glass upon which are pressed scenes of historical interest, and these are of especial interest to American collectors. Examples of authentic milk glass are also highly prized—although there are so many reproductions of milk glass that what you do find will probably be merely another reproduction. Yet there is always the chance that you have found an authentic piece—and if you have, it belongs in the hands of the collectors.

There are also in America many types of European glass—shipped here as gifts, wedding presents, etc., or sometimes even for the commercial market—which are worth your time and effort. These would include the fabulous Bohemian glass of the 1500's; English crystal glass of the late 1600's; and the smoky blue glass of Waterford, Ireland, which was produced for over a century.

The list of types of glass to watch for is endless, and any piece of glass, if it is old enough, rare enough, and beautiful enough, should be investigated by the treasure hunter.

THE pastor of the little church steps down from the pulpit and hands one red rose—the year's annual rent—to the descendant of the Lord of the Manor. Feudal times? Europe in the Middle Ages? No! For the time is now and the place is a little town in Pennsylvania.

It is a strange thing to happen in our days, in our country, but it is so. It is the strange story which begins with two words: Glass—and Stiegel!

The words Stiegel and glass are synonymous with treasured glass—and the treasure hunter will do well to remember it. If he has what he thinks might be a piece of Stiegel ware I might suggest, as a reference, the book *Stiegel Glass* by William Hunter, with introduction and notes by Helen McKearin, 1950, New York, Dover Publications, Inc. This book may be used by the treasure hunter to familiarize himself with Stiegel ware as he searches for it, and to check what he has found against known items of Stiegel's.

One thing which the treasure hunter will soon discover is that there are certain colors which are of more value than other, more common, shades of Stiegel glass. Cobalt blue and amethyst are the two colors to especially look for, because these are the most unique.

Any example of Stiegel glass, however, is worth something to the treasure hunter. Stiegel glass of any kind is a rare find. There is, however, one pitfall open to the Stiegel hunter: there were many "Stiegel types" of glassware made both here and abroad.

But there are many authentic Stiegel items to watch for. He made many types and kinds of glass objects, from bottles, jugs, and salt cellars, to mustard pots, decanters and tumblers, and even window glass.

When searching for this glassware, it is also important to remember the age of the glass. The Stiegel glassworks were open from 1763 to 1774, making any glassware made in this factory very old by American standards.

Very old—and very fine—for Heinrich Wilhelm Stiegel did nothing halfway. In his factory he employed the very best of foreign workmen, and he also did something which was unheard of in that day. For his workmen he built a whole town—and for their education and happiness he built a church.

He called his little town Manheim. Today, Manheim, Pa., remembers Stiegel as one of its earliest and most illustrious citizens. The town remembers Stiegel as a man who lived in his own way—a way which harked back to feudal times. Manheim remembers Stiegel as the man who rode in fabulous coaches and lived like the old-time nobility. It remembers him as a man who loved riches and fine and expensive things.

He called himself Baron Stiegel. Today, no one knows for sure whether the title was authentic, but Stiegel certainly lived like a Baron.

It is known definitely that he was born in Germany and that he came to America as a very young man, arriving in Philadelphia in 1750. Very little else is known about him. We do know, however, that he became famous and wealthy, and that he loved his wealth, and that he spent money so lavishly that his extravagances eventually broke him.

He lost everything, and he died a forgotten man. Even his grave was not considered important enough to remember.

By the time the people of Manheim awoke to the fact that one of their most illustrious citizens had died—and that he should be remembered by them—it was too late, and his grave has not been located to this day.

Even though Manheim forgot Stiegel as he lay dying, Stiegel remembered Manheim. As one of his last acts he willed a parcel of ground he owned in Manheim to the congregation of the Zion Lutheran Church. This was the little church that Stiegel himself had named.

Today Manheim—belatedly—remembers Stiegel in a ceremony which is known as the "Feast of the Roses," held on the first Sunday of June every year. One red rose is handed, by the pastor of the church, to a descendant of the "Baron" Stiegel.

This red rose is the year's rent for the use of the lot which Stiegel willed to the church. This annual payment of a rose was stipulated in the will which Stiegel himself had made in that grand and feudal manner which he loved so well.

Yet even without his "Feast of the Roses" Stiegel would be remembered as long as collectors search for specimens of fine and treasured glass.

The treasure hunter will do well to remember him, too.

XXV

Treasure in the House

From Clocks to Stoves

NOT too long ago an old-fashioned so-called grandfather's clock, made in the latter part of the eighteenth century, was valued at over one thousand dollars.

Almost all of the old American clocks have some value. Even the old pine mantel clocks of a century later can be worth from $80 to $90 apiece, depending on condition, age, etc.

One name to remember in clock hunting is Seth Thomas, who began his own "clock factory" shortly after the beginning of the nineteenth century.

When the company was started, approximately twenty men worked there—and they were paid once a year! From 1813 to 1837 they made such things as looking-glass clocks and hall clocks, all of them with wooden movements, but in 1838 brass movements were introduced and in 1860 perpetual-calendar clocks were made by the company.

One fact worth remembering in your search for old Seth Thomas clocks is that labels on Seth Thomas clocks read "Plymouth Hollow" until 1866, when the name appearing on the clock labels as town of manufacture was changed to "Thomaston" in honor of Seth Thomas.

Also watch for the American clocks of Eli Terry, a contemporary of Thomas'. Nor should you forget the European clocks which were brought to America by the settlers of the eighteenth and nineteenth centuries. Some of these clocks date as far back as the 1600's

—and their value depends on their age and their condition. There are English clocks, French clocks and Swiss clocks, all of them worth watching for.

Also do not forget the smaller items of this art—the watch of yesterday which your ancestor proudly displayed to his friends as he entertained them in his home. These watches, some of them dating back to the 1500's, were brought to America—only to be lost in the vicissitudes of time and war and cross-country pioneer treks.

Watches from all nations and from the past four centuries have value—if you can find them. So take another look at that old watch that has been in the family for so many generations. It might well be that in your case it is really a time for treasure.

Perhaps, while looking for grandpa's old watch, you might run across other objects which today are worth something—like old inkwells which can be worth $100 apiece or even more, if they are of fine workmanship, old enough, and rare enough.

Or you might find an old piece of silver dating back two or more centuries. All of it has value, especially silverware which is hall-marked (that is, marked by the silversmith on the back or on the bottom), perhaps as long ago as the 1500's.

Or you might find old candlesticks, some perhaps of silver, very rare and very valuable. Or perhaps hand-worked, wooden candlesticks worth only a few dollars or so—but all of them worth something.

Or early American lamps of all kinds, including examples of the early "Betty" lamps, some of them maybe imported for use in our early colonies. Any old lamp can have value if it is old enough, rare enough, and in fine enough condition.

One item to watch for, although harder to find in your trips through the second-hand stores, are the chandeliers of yesterday. Sometimes such items are overlooked by the second-hand-store owners because they are unable to date them—and unable to evaluate them. Therefore they just might sell you a valuable one for next to nothing.

This, of course, is no reflection on second-hand-store dealers, only an observation that many times they have neither the opportunities nor the time to evaluate all the items which go through their hands.

This, however, is not true of the antique dealer—who can evaluate any old chandelier which you might find. If you are lucky enough, you might even locate chandeliers of rock crystal from the periods of Louis XIV and Louis XV before you leave the second-hand store.

Any old light is worth something. Even an old tavern light, if in good enough condition, can be worth from $70 to $80. Ruby-glass lights can be worth anything from a hundred to several hundred dollars, depending as always on age, etc.

Or, while browsing through the same second-hand store, you might run across hatracks, some of them not even a hundred years old, which can be worth from $50 to $100 apiece.

Or you might find a stove—but not just any stove. This is one that even the experts have searched for and failed to find! For this is the Franklin stove, invented by Benjamin Franklin. The stove in question of course would be Franklin's own stove, and not a later, modified version.

The experts have searched everywhere for this stove—but so far without success. Perhaps you might succeed where even the experts have failed. It has been known to happen before!

Yet even one of the later modified versions can be worth something. A so-called Franklin stove from the nineteenth century can be worth around $100.

From the stove to the sink is not a very long way. For even a sink can have value—if it is old enough and fine enough. A Pennsylvania Dutch dry sink, dated in the late eighteenth century, can be worth a couple of hundred dollars—if you can find it. Or a washstand from a century later can be worth from $50 to $75.

Even the doorstop holding open the store door might be worth a few dollars if it is old enough. Anything you see in the second-hand stores, in your attic, or in your cellar might be worth something—if you know what you are looking for.

If it is of fine craftsmanship and if it is lovely—whether it is a clock, a stove or a sink—if it has been made by a master craftsman and is old enough, then it is worth investigating.

Do not ever again pass up that old junk clock, the old trashy sink, or that funny-looking old lamp. They may not be junk after all. They might be collectors' items.

XXVI

FURNITURE

Chippendale to Franklin

THERE is a magic name in the world of furniture—so magic that even the furniture just made in the style for which he was famous is worth a fortune. His name is Thomas Chippendale.

He has been called the greatest of all the world's furniture makers. Today, if you can find anything in the "Chippendale" manner, if it is old enough and in fine enough condition, it can be worth a fortune.

A Chippendale desk can be worth as much as $36,000—or even more. Chippendale chairs can be worth $200 or $300 apiece, and some of them have been valued as high as $500 or $600 each.

Any Chippendale table is worth hundreds of dollars—and anything else that can be authenticated as Chippendale is worth a great deal.

One woman, at least according to one story, found this out by trying to sell some old "junk." She thought it was junk until the dealers saw it and labeled it "treasure." There was some old silver, dating back two centuries. And the furniture? Part of it was Sheraton —and part of it was Chippendale!

When they were through evaluating her old "junk" they paid her $100,000 for it!

While you are gasping at the great amount she received for her old Chippendale and silver, do not forget the name of Sheraton, for this is another name in furniture which carries with it both magic and dollars for the finder.

Sheraton was the eighteenth-century furniture designer who never even owned his own shop. He did not even make a good living for himself. He was a jack of all trades: preacher, teacher, writer—and furniture designer.

Today a Sheraton cabinet can be sold for around $500—if you can find it. Or one of his tables can be worth $1,000 or more, if it is in fine condition.

Perhaps that old piece of furniture which you found may be neither Chippendale nor Sheraton. It might be Hepplewhite! It might even be a Hepplewhite Secretaire bookcase worth $1,000.

Or it might be a piece of Adams furniture worth, certainly, a great deal. These pieces of lost furniture could be anywhere! When looking for lost treasures of this kind, there is no limit as to where they might be.

In your attic, your cellar, the second-hand store—or even in your yard, like the ten-thousand-pound, inlaid-marble, sixteenth-century table which was found in the yard of an English house wrecker.

Anywhere at all! And they could have traveled thousands of miles before they came to rest in your neighborhood second-hand store! The inlaid-marble table had originally been designed for a Roman palace—but the yard in which it was rediscovered belonged to a house wrecker!

The piece of furniture you find may have traveled all the way across the ocean to some family who liked European imported goods. Only to be lost again through war or misfortune—or by simply being thrown out by descendants of the original owners, because they did not know what they had.

What they threw out may even have been a Louis XV table worth thousands of dollars. Perhaps it may have been fine enough to have brought in a sale almost as much as one Louis XV table which was sold recently. This particular table was sold for $100,000!

So take another look at that old "junky table" in the attic. It could be Louis XV. Or it might be only a Provincial table, made contemporarily with, but in imitation of, the Louis XV style. Yet even if it is Provincial, it would still be worth hundreds of dollars.

Or it could be a Louis XV chair worth thousands of dollars—or it could be a chair of the later period, called Louis XVI and still be worth over $1,000. Or a Louis XVI table worth $5,000 or more.

From a later period, when Napoleon sat on the throne of France, you might find furniture of the Directoire and Empire periods, worth several hundred dollars apiece.

Or you might find items of the so-called Regency type, chairs worth hundreds of dollars apiece, or sofas of the same period, also worth hundreds of dollars each. Or a Regency stand worth $500 or more. Also watch for Queen Anne furniture, some of it worth many thousands of dollars.

Any piece of furniture, if it is old enough and rare enough, can be worth something. Like the miniatures which were so prevalent at one time. One story is that they were made for children. Another story is that they were made by apprentice furniture makers to show the quality of their work. But for whatever reason they were made, they are worth something today. A miniature chest of drawers, for example, is worth from $60 to $70.

Even such odd items of furniture as *papier mâché* tables and chairs are worth something. A *papier mâché* chair can be worth a couple of hundred dollars—and a *papier mâché* table can be worth even more.

Whatever it is, if it is of fine craftsmanship, is old enough, and has the proper lines, it is valuable.

It takes an expert, of course, to properly evaluate a piece of old furniture, but you can learn the different styles of furniture and therefore know what to look for. Your librarian can give you books with pictures of the various styles. Most encyclopedias have pictures showing examples of the different makes and styles of furniture. You can go to your local museums and see examples of fine furniture. Remembering what you have seen there, you will know what to look for the next time you go treasure hunting for lost furniture.

When you find a piece that looks old to you, look for wear on the corners and on the bottoms of the legs. Watch for old-fashioned nails or wooden pegs. And just plain beauty! For there is nothing quite so beautiful as an antique chair or table. Or if you are the kind who does not like antiques, then look again and imagine the hundreds or thousands of dollars which you can sell it for! And it will look just as beautiful to you as it will to the collector who will gladly dig deep in his pocket for cold, hard cash.

A DUNCAN PHYFE table can be worth almost $1,000—if you can find it!

So can any other piece of furniture labeled as connected with the Scotsman Phyfe, who came to America to become one of our most famous furniture designers. Watch for any piece of his furniture—for, if authenticated, it is worth a small fortune.

The value of a piece of furniture, however, is sometimes overshadowed by the historical importance of it. Such as the furniture made by John Alden! Today, where are all of the pieces which he must have made for his Priscilla? Some of it, perhaps, in the museums, but some of it, perhaps, in your attic—if you would only take the time and trouble to look!

When John Alden died, he was an old man of eighty-eight, and surely during his lifetime he must have produced many items—which you might possibly find if you are lucky.

In looking for furniture by John Alden, however, do not overlook the furniture of the rest of the early settlers. Any furniture belonging to or made by any of the Pilgrims who came over on the Mayflower has value today.

Remember the Pilgrim names of Carver and Brewster, for furniture connected with their names has value. It has not been too many years since a Carver chair was sold for $1,000.

Or remember the chair made by another of our early Americans—the legendary rocking chair of Benjamin Franklin. The story goes that Franklin invented the rocking chair because he was uncomfortable in his old straight chair. He solved his problem by putting rockers on it.

The story is a legend, and it may or may not be true! Franklin's so-called rocking chair may have been confused, in the story, with his fan chair, which he did invent and which is missing.

Certainly we know that the fan chair existed, because at least one person saw it—and recorded what he saw. In 1787, the Reverend Dr. Manasseh Cutler, visiting Franklin, saw an article of furniture which he describes as "his (Franklin's) great armchair, with rockers, and a large fan placed over it, with which he fans himself, keeps off the flies, etc., while he sits reading, with only a small motion of the foot. . . ."

Every museum curator and every collector in America would grab at this chair—if you could find it.

Anything made in the early part of American history can have value, if old enough, fine enough, and rare enough. Chests have been known to bring from $500 to over $5,000. Cupboards can be worth several hundred dollars. Tables can be worth a couple of hundred dollars. Anything from this period is worth investigating.

Also, while investigating furniture from this period, do not forget the furniture of the later era named for Victoria of England. Pieces in this style are becoming rarer and more expensive by the day.

Already some of the finer examples have been valued at several hundred dollars apiece, and as the fad for Victoriana increases, so will the value of each piece.

So do not throw away your great-aunt's old chair or sofa which you have been hiding in the attic. Take it out and have another look at it.

Furniture which you think is junk might turn out to be fortune in disguise. You could have anything from an early Phyfe to the rocking chair of Benjamin Franklin.

XXVII

Diamonds All Around You

Where to Look for Them

A FARMER'S children kept finding pretty pebbles in the yard —pebbles which they thought were pretty playthings. Their mother gave one of them to a neighbor, who sold the pebble for several pounds—and the word was out. Diamonds had been discovered in South Africa!

Many years later, in faraway Brazil, two farmers walked along the path of a dry river bed. A stone glinted in the sunlight and they passed it by. Later, his curiosity aroused, one of them returned. The stone turned out to be the seven-hundred-and-twenty-six-and-a-half-carat Vargas diamond.

Fabulous finds, but no one seems to think it so strange, because the finds were made in other countries. Yet here in the United States, diamonds have been found in the past—and will be again if you know where to look for them.

In 1906 a farmer in Arkansas was doing his plowing—and uncovered a two-and-three-quarter-carat diamond. This was the beginning of the Arkansas diamond field.

Today our Arkansas field is limited in output—but while it was in full operation more than fifty thousand diamonds were taken out, the largest of them weighing forty carats. Today, however, you can still find diamonds in Arkansas, because there is a place called the "Crater of Diamonds" near Murfreesboro which is open to the public and where anyone can hunt for diamonds.

Only a few years ago a housewife on vacation went to the Crater of Diamonds and found a fifteen-and-one-half-carat diamond. It was named the "Star of Arkansas." A couple of years later a man and his wife found a three-carat diamond worth over two thousand dollars. And there are more diamonds in the Crater of Diamonds— waiting for you to find them. If they are less than five carats you get to keep them, but if they are over five you must give a percentage to the people who own the property. Still, this is treasure. Who would not be willing to share a percentage of a ten- or twelve-carat diamond—just for the right to look for it!

But there are other places right here in the United States where you can find diamonds. In 1928, in the town of Peterstown, West Virginia, a father and son set up a game of horseshoes in a vacant lot. It was a game of horseshoes which they will never forget—for during the course of that game they accidentally discovered the "Punch Jones," a thirty-four-carat diamond.

The West Virginia diamond is a little different from the Arkansas diamond. For this is a glacier diamond, swept downwards thousands of years ago by the onslaught of the glaciers, the big ice that swept everything before it—including diamonds.

There are many states wherein glacier diamonds have been found, but the point, of course, is that the glaciers swept them away from some particular place—a mother lode, probably somewhere in Canada.

This mother lode has never been found, and its extent is anyone's guess. Perhaps the big ice swept all the diamonds before it—or, again, we may have another Kimberley in our northern back yard. We never will know, until some treasure hunter finds it.

Another Kimberley sounds fantastic, yet by tracing the paths of the glaciers and by knowing that glacier diamonds have been found in those paths, we know that there is at least a possibility of a rich and fabulous mother lode somewhere in Canada, probably in the Hudson Bay region.

Glacier diamonds have been found in many states, particularly of course in the Great Lakes states, but even in West Virginia it is wise to watch for them. You might find another Punch Jones!

Glacier diamonds, however, are not the only diamonds to watch for. In California alone over two hundred diamonds have been "accidentally" found by men who were gold mining. They turned up during ordinary gold panning operations.

Diamonds have been found from one end of the United States to the other—in a country where most people might not even glance twice at the shiny pebble they saw while they were on their Sunday picnic or summer vacation. But remember the two Brazilian farmers who passed by the Vargas diamond. Only one of them was curious enough to go back and look it over again.

A diamond of gem quality can be worth $1,000 a carat, but the lesser-quality diamond, the industrial diamond, is so badly needed by industry that, if you could find them a good source of industrial diamonds, they would welcome you with open arms.

It takes the industrial diamond to successfully operate many modern production plants. Today, our need for the home production of industrial diamonds has become so acute that the United States Bureau of Mines has begun a project to prospect for them.

More romantic than industrial diamonds, of course, is the treasure hunter's hope of finding a magnificent, large, gem stone— but first he must be able to recognize one if he should find it. A diamond in the rough does not look like the lovely, sparkling gem that we see in a jeweler's window.

True, it is as hard; but it is not as pretty. It has a glassy or frosty appearance, and it sometimes feels greasy to the fingers as you rub it, and many times it looks just like certain types of quartz. Yet, while both quartz and diamond will scratch glass, the diamond will scratch the quartz.

Diamonds, to be gem stones, should be free of all blemishes or flaws. They are clear stones, yet a deeply colored stone may become a stone of great value—like the Blue Hope diamond.

When you are looking for diamonds, do not throw away frosted or glassy looking stones because of their odd color. Diamonds come in all colors. They can be yellow or green, blue or pink, brown or red, gray or black.

Any color—and almost anywhere. Watch for them in the dirt, imbedded in rocks, in sand, in the gravel of dried-up river beds, and in the rippling brooks. Diamonds have been found in many such California streams leading down from the Sierra Nevada. They have been found in the Great Lakes region, on the Pacific coast, and in the Atlantic-Piedmont region.

You can look for them almost anywhere. More specifically you can look for them in the following areas:

Alabama: Lee, Shelby Counties

Arkansas: Pike County: Murfreesboro

California: Amador County: Indian Gulch, Volcano
Butte County: Cherokee Flats, Oroville and Yankee Hill
Del Norte County: Smith River
Eldorado County: Placerville and Webber Hill
Nevada County: French Corral
Plumas County: Spanish Creek and Gopher Hill
Trinity County: Trinity River
Tulare County: Alpine Creek

Georgia: White County: Harshaw Mine, Acooche Valley
Clayton County: Morrow Station
Hall County: Gainesville

Idaho: Ada County: Diamond basin

Indiana: Morgan County: Martinsville
Brown County: Lick Creek near Morgantown

Kentucky: Russell County: Cabin Fork Creek

Michigan: Cass County: Dowagiac

Montana: Glacier County: Nelson Hill near Blackfoot

North Carolina: Burke County: Brindletown Creek Ford
Cleveland County: King's Mountain
Franklin County: Portis mine
Lincoln County: Cottage Home
McDowell County: Headwaters of Muddy Creek, Dysortville
Mecklenburg County: Todd Branch
Rutherford County: Twetty's mine

Ohio: Clermont County: Milford near Cincinnati

South Carolina: Spartanburg County

Tennessee: Roane County: Clinch River near Union Crossroads

Texas: Walker County: Huntsville

Virginia: Chesterfield County: Manchester

West Virginia: Monroe County: Peterstown

Wisconsin: Dane County: Oregon
Ozaukee County: Saukville
Pierce County: Plum creek
Racine County: Burlington
Washington County: Kohlsville
Waukesha County: Eagle

XXVIII

FOUR-ALARM TREASURE

Fire Marks from the Days of Yesteryear

DO you know that a fire mark can be worth a thousand dollars? Or do you even know what it is?

Have you ever looked at the side of an old building—and seen a plate or plaque nailed securely to the wall? Have you ever wondered what it was? Well, chances are good that it was a fire mark, telling firemen that this building was insured by the company whose name or emblem was illustrated on the plaque.

The fire mark was placed on the outside of a building so that the fire brigade—and anyone else interested—would know that the building was insured and by which company.

Fire marks were always placed on the *outside* of a building. They are usually to be found on an old building between the first and second floors rather than on the ground floor, because this prevented the fire mark from being destroyed or removed by pranksters or children.

However, in towns along the rivers, the treasure hunter must search as high as six stories up for the fire mark, which was placed so high because of the floods which are common in some river towns. Located well above the water line of the highest possible flood stage, the fire marks were in plain view at all times and the firemen could easily tell who insured the building.

Fire marks were first used in Europe, where they have been

known for almost three hundred years, but in both Europe and America each company adopted its own particular fire mark.

In Europe, in the early days of their history, the fire marks identified property insured by a particular company, so that the insurance companies, which had their own fire brigades, could put out fires on properties which were marked by their own particular fire mark.

American fire marks were first used in the 1750's although even before then America had organized methods of fire fighting. In 1696 bucket brigades were formed. In 1718 the first fire engine was brought over from London; and in 1721 we find a public chimney sweep appointed, although this was in the line of fire prevention rather than fire fighting.

In 1735 the first fire brigade was formed, and in 1752 the first American fire insurance company was formed. In America, the fire brigades knew that the insurance company, whose mark was on a building, would reward the fire brigade which successfully put out the fire. And if two or more brigades showed up to put out the fire, many times fights broke out among the firemen, with bloody noses and black eyes attesting to their claim that their brigade, and their brigade alone, was the one which put out the fire.

Many times the fights took place—with each brigade using their fists to prove that they got there first with the best men and the best equipment—while the fire raged on. Sometimes the building burned down before the fire fighters stopped fighting each other.

If the brigades arrived at a building which did not have a fire mark—they turned around and went home, and the building burned merrily down.

The use of the fire mark has died away until today it is an almost forgotten piece of early Americana—but not to the collector of fire marks, for to him the tradition lives on.

American fire marks have been made of tin, cast iron, and lead. Fire marks have also been made of brass, copper and zinc. And some comparatively recent fire marks were made of porcelain or enamel upon iron.

Probably one of the most interesting searches for lost treasures ever made was the search made for the first fire mark put out by the Insurance Company of North America. It was "A wavy star of six points, cast in lead and mounted on a wooden shield."

The first fire mark of this company—the star design—was issued in 1794, but later other designs replaced this one. But it was the "star" which every collector wanted.

In 1914, it was believed that no star designs were in existence. In 1915 it was believed that the star variety had been lost forever. In 1928 the star design was still believed to have been all destroyed.

Yet a year later, on an old building on Pace Street, near Second, in the city of Philadelphia, a collector noticed an unusual stain on the face of the building. Being a collector, he noticed immediately that the stain was the same size and shape as the shield which records said was the shield of the star design.

He located the owner of the building—and then the owner's father, and then the owner's grandfather. Finally, after many questions and searchings, the shield was found—in the hands of a carpenter.

Believing himself, happily, in possession of the lost "star," imagine the collector's disappointment when he discovered that while the shield was the right size and shape, the design nailed to it was another design entirely—one which was not rare at all.

But, not ready to give up, he carefully examined what he had and discovered, underneath the not-so-rare fire mark, an outline—the outline of a star.

Careful questioning brought out the facts that the star had been sold years before to a second-hand dealer from Baltimore. Then the search began in earnest. Every antique and second-hand store in Baltimore was searched and their managers and owners questioned with regard to the star.

Finally, on the outskirts of the city, the star was found. It had been gathering dust for years on the shelves of the shop. Even then, however, the collector was not satisfied. First he applied chemical tests to prove the age of the star. Then he tried the star against the shield—and it fitted, "nail hole for nail hole, line for line!"

Today, that star is with the collection of the Insurance Company of North America Companies, and it is exhibited at 1600 Arch street in Philadelphia, which now has not one star design but two.

C. A. Palmer, of that company, states almost sadly, ". . . this company's first mark, the six-pointed lead star on wood, is so rare . . . there being only two in existence that we know of, that from a monetary point of view, no amount of money would produce another one, and fortunately one of these rare marks was donated to us, whereas the other cost us $500."

The treasure hunter's challenge here is obvious—find another "star."

The value of fire marks, as in coin collecting, is based on rarity and condition. Rare marks are worth from $200 to $1,000 apiece, depending on age and condition. There are certain lone fire marks which are unique, however, and if a new, unique mark were to be discovered, it would be quite valuable.

Below are listed fire marks which are considered rare, worth on an average around $200 apiece.

> **Philadelphia Contributionship:** (1) Fancy or scalloped design shield—four interlocking hands, issued about 1765. (2) Shield has rounded top and bevel edge, issue of 1774. (3) Shield is plain edged board, issued about 1776. (4) Much smaller than above, issue of 1815, oddly shaped plaque. (5) Issue of 1819, small hands.
>
> **Mutual Assurance Company for Insuring Houses from Loss by Fire, Philadelphia:** (1) Design of the "Green Tree"—dated 1784—shows a leaden tree on a bevelled-edge shield of wood. (2) Absence of bevelled edge, issue of 1797. (3) First of the elliptical wooden shields, issued in 1799. (4) Issue of 1803, shield much smaller than the first oval—last wooden mark issued by the company. (5) The first all-iron mark of the "Green Tree" and largest of its iron varieties—this one measures thirteen inches from top to bottom. Known as the "large flat back," issue of 1805. (6) Issue of 1806—known as "small flat back"—the second iron mark issued by this company. (7) Not more than three dozen of this squatty iron variety are known to have been issued, dates from 1827.
>
> **Insurance Company of North America:** (1) Leaden eagle on a wooden plaque. The marks dated 1794 are the famous "star" fire marks but after December 26, 1796, the insured had a choice of this leaden eagle or the six-pointed star. (2) Copper eagle rising from a cloud. This mark has a rolled edge and came into use just after 1800. Not more than six specimens are known to exist. (3) Iron eagle, differing slightly from the copper eagle. This mark was first issued in 1830 and has a beaded edge.
>
> **Fire Association of Philadelphia:** (1) Fire Association mark dating 1817. Flat and made of iron, with a full stream of water gushing from a hose attached to an old-time fire plug. The letters "F.A." were gilded, as were the plug and hose. The grass at the base of the hydrant was green. (2) Also an extremely flat, iron variety, except that water is not gushing from the hose. This is the only mark made by the Fire Association with a short hose ending to

the right of the center of the mark; issue of 1825. (3) Made of lead; issued 1857. (4) Made of brass. Only twelve issued; some have many sets of numbers in gilt; dates about 1859. Rarest of all issues of this company.

Hope Mutual Insurance Company of Philadelphia: (1) Issued in 1854, an oval iron casting with beaded edge, showing in center a figure of "Hope" resting on an anchor.

United Firemen's Insurance Company of Philadelphia: (1) Issue of 1860; very large, heavy iron casting. Has three holes for attaching to houses, whereas later marks have the regulation two holes.

City Insurance Company of Cincinnati, Ohio: (1) This company went out of business before 1850; the fire mark was issued about 1846. It is a large, iron casting, showing an old-type fire engine with crew. The mark is distinctive by reason of its very fancy shape.

Union Insurance Company, Charleston, S.C.: (1) Founded on June 17, 1807, the company retired about 1839. The fire mark, an oval casting, tells the story of fire insurance. On one side, a building in flames, on the other, a new building. All Charleston fire marks are rare, as the town was partially destroyed by fire on many occasions between 1700 and 1900.

Mutual Insurance Company, Charleston, S.C.: (1) Issued about 1798; an oval, iron casting, the mark shows a guardian angel hovering over a city, sprinkling water on fire. First iron fire mark made in America.

United States Insurance Company of Baltimore, Md.: (1) Issued in 1834; oblong, almost square, iron casting.

Fire Insurance Company of New Orleans, La.: (1) This mark has, in both design and initials, a most striking resemblance to the mark of the Fire Association of Philadelphia. Oval, iron casting, issued in 1806, a year after the founding of the company.

Mobile Fire Department Insurance Company, Mobile, Ala.: (1) Company founded in 1866; retired in 1879. The mark is an iron casting showing a fireman's hat and company's initials in raised letters.

Baltimore Equitable Society, Baltimore, Md.: (1) The first fire mark of this company, issued in 1794, was handmade of tile on wood. No specimen of this mark has been found. (2) Issued about 1795. The iron casting of the clasped hands is mounted on the original wooden plaque. (3) Issued about 1820; iron casting on a wooden plaque. Index finger on the hand is much longer than in any other marks put out by this company. Cuffs are more pronounced and lacy than in the issue of 1795. Probably many valuable specimens were lost in the great Baltimore fire of 1904.

Mutual Insurance Company of Washington County, Hagerstown, Md.: (1) Issued in 1847. Iron casting, oblong with raised border. Shows hands clasped and raised initials of company.

Associated Firemen's Insurance Company of Baltimore, Md.: (1) Issued in 1848; of cast iron with rounded oval edge, very large and heavy. Mark shows a fireman blowing a horn and holding a burning brand.

Firemen's Insurance Company of Baltimore, Md.: (1) Mark, issued about 1840. Wheels of pumper have twelve spokes. Loop at top for hanging is plain. (2) Largest mark, issued about 1855. Loop at top for hanging is plain and round. Wheels of pumper have six spokes.

Firemen's Insurance Company of the District of Columbia: (1) Issued about 1838. Large, thick, iron casting, very heavy. Very similar to mark of the Firemen's of Baltimore, above.

Hartford County Mutual Fire Insurance Company: (1) Issued in 1831; made of tin, it is oval and convex.

Clay Fire and Marine Insurance Company, Newport, Ky.: (1) Issued in 1789; odd-shaped, iron casting.

Associated Firemen's Insurance Company of Pittsburgh, Pa.: (1) Issued about 1851; cast iron, showing a standing figure of a fireman, fully equipped, blowing a horn. In his left hand is a wrench for tapping the fire plug.

Penn Fire Insurance Company of Pittsburgh, Pa.: (1) Issued in 1841; it is of cast iron, showing the bust of William Penn.

Firemen's Insurance Company of Pittsburgh, Pa.: (1) Issued in 1834; it is an oblong, iron casting showing an old fire engine.

Western Mutual Fire and Marine Insurance Company, St. Louis, Mo.: (1) Issued in 1857; oval mark, showing clasped hands and name of company in raised letters.

Franklin Insurance Company, St. Louis, Mo.: (1) Issued in 1855; made of zinc. Has the name of the company and city on it.

Laclede Mutual Insurance Company, St. Louis, Mo.: (1) Issued in 1859; small, oval, tin mark. Light in weight, name of company in raised letters, clasped hands in center.

Washington Mutual Insurance Company, Boston, Mass.: (1) Issued in 1844; made of brass, oblong with raised border. Size 8½″ x 4¼″.

Protection Mutual Fire Insurance Company, Thomaston, Maine: (1) Issued in 1849; an oval, tin plate with the company's initials shown.

Insurance Company of Florida, Jacksonville, Fla.: (1) Issued in 1841; entirely of wood. Bears the letters "I.F." in high relief.

Mutual Assurance Company of New York City: (1) Issued 1787; of heavy tin, oval in shape. Painted black with "Mutual Assurance" in gilt letters. Number of the policy on a space beneath. (Only two specimens are extant today.)

Niagara District Mutual Fire Insurance Company, Niagara Falls, N.Y.: (1) Issued in 1836; a small, heavy, iron casting with very prominently raised, clasped hands. The name of the company runs around the edge of the mark, forming a border. Date of founding of company is also given.

Milwaukee Mechanics', Milwaukee, Wis.: (1) Issued in 1853; oval, iron casting with beaded edge, name of company showing plainly on front in raised letters.

Home Insurance Company, New Haven, Conn.: (1) Company lasted from 1859 to 1871. The fire mark is a thick, iron casting of oval shape. It shows the figure of a fireman and an old-time fire engine and plug in bold relief.

Protection Fire Insurance Company, Charleston, W.Va.: (1) Exact date of the organization of this company is not known; it went out of business in 1894 and undoubtedly was an old company. The mark is an oblong, iron casting showing raised eagle and name of company. A few years ago a large portion of Charleston was destroyed by fire, and many of these marks were lost.

Citizens' Fire, Marine and Life Insurance Company, Wheeling, W.Va.: (1) Issued in 1856; very odd-shaped casting, with name of company in raised letters.

Peabody Fire and Marine Insurance Company, Wheeling, West Va.: (1) Issued in 1869; a heavy, iron casting; fancy, oblong shape.

Perhaps, if you are lucky, you will find a fire mark similar to the ones described above or even another design which is even rarer and which might be in the $1,000 bracket.

XXIX

Dead Whales, Hair Nets—and a Dash of Beauty

Women's Follies through the Ages

A WOMAN will do anything to enhance her beauty, even if it means wading out into the ocean to drag in the contents of the intestinal canal of a dead whale.

Each year more and more treasure seekers scour long stretches of our beaches trying to locate the gray smelly substance that is ambergris. Most of the time the substance found is nothing more than vegetable wax or soap from passing ships, but the one find in a thousand will be the gray lumps which are ambergris—that fantastic substance so necessary for the retention of the delicate odors of perfumes—without which perfume would be of little use to the woman who treasures it so highly.

The smell of ambergris, as found in the ocean—if you are lucky enough to find it—has been likened both to musk and to a sweet earthy odor. Often it will contain the beaks of cuttlefish, and this is one way of telling whether or not the substance you have found is actually ambergris—or somebody's left-over soap.

Usually found in small amounts, it sometimes appears as a great glob weighing as much as five hundred pounds!

In ancient days, ambergris was used for medicinal purposes and was purported to be the excrement of the sperm whale. Today we know that at its origin the ambergris is enclosed in the intestinal canal of the sperm whale. Also, it *must* come from a diseased whale. It is for this reason that ambergris is so rare. One whale is capable of producing hundreds of pounds of this substance, but, then, how many sick whales are there?

It is this scarcity of ambergris which makes the price paid for it so high—in recent years reaching about $20 a pound, or $2,000 per one hundred pounds, or $10,000 for five hundred pounds. Obviously well worth watching for—and even wading for.

Yet there are other items connected with perfume that can be found without getting your feet wet. Among them the cones which were set into the wigs worn by the women of ancient Egypt. These cones contained perfume and would, today, be considered items of great historical interest.

The Romans also had their own methods of filling the air with scent. The women of Rome carried silver and golden nets into which were placed small balls of amber, and when the amber was rubbed, it threw off fragrance into the air—amber balls worth watching for.

Besides perfume, there are other treasures used by women of the past to enhance their beauty, and among them are examples of embroidery.

There have been times in our history when embroidery ranked as high in prestige as the great paintings of the day. Some examples of this ancient art have survived—and they may be waiting for you to find them. From ancient China, watch for the silk, brocade-embroidered robes of the women who lived under the ancient Manchus. Watch for the white robes of the ancient Greeks, robes embroidered in reds, blues, yellows, and other colors.

In earlier times, during the Middle Ages, embroidery was so popular that monasteries and convents had special rooms where nothing else was done except that work. The patterns showed a Byzantine influence—fine and lovely workmanship for the treasure hunter to locate, if he can.

From the thirteen to the fifteen hundreds, Europe was a center for some of the most exquisite pieces of embroidered work the world had ever known, lovely things to clothe the most beautiful ladies of the land.

Even the men got into the embroidery act, in the seventeen hundreds, when Louis XV ruled France and it was fashionable for men of the court to appear in handsomely embroidered coats. These coats are today well worth your search, keeping in mind that some of the most beautiful of these had been sent all the way to China for their embroidery work—although the design of the embroidery was distinctly European.

Rarity, age, historical association, and fine workmanship are the criteria upon which is based the evaluation of any piece of embroidery. Let us hope that the piece of embroidery which has been in your family for so many years can meet the rigid standards of these pieces of worked cloth which are considered as great art in their own right.

But embroidery is not the only cloth to watch for, beautiful though it is. Ancient Japanese brocade robes dating to the late 1500's would be museum pieces if you could find good examples of them. Also from ancient Japan come robes which were decorated with gold and silver foil, sometimes even with glass. How heavy these must have been for the women who wore them, especially since the Japanese ladies wore as many as twenty articles of dress at once, one over the other.

From ancient Byzantium, watch for cloth of gold. They wore fantastic garments, from patterned silk to cloth, into which gold was woven; many of them are museum pieces.

In feudal times, the noble ladies of the land wore cloth woven with gold. They called it aureotextile. Sometimes they wore aureoclavi, which means brocaded with gold. Women's clothing from this period is always worth watching for, especially since it became so fabulous that laws were passed limiting the extravagances to which women might go in having their clothes decorated.

From the later period of the Renaissance there are many items of clothing to watch for—brocades and velvets and silks. Robes were lined with crimson silk, or sometimes with ermine and sable.

Fashion was so important at one time that fashion dolls were made especially to display the latest thing in milady's fashion world. This was in the late thirteen hundreds, when each year the city of Venice sent to Paris for a fashion doll which, on Ascension Day, was placed on display in Piazza San Marco.

Whether it is a fashion doll, a piece of golden embroidery, or a gray and smelly lump of ambergris, it is treasure—if you can find it.

TRULY the beauty of womankind offers an unlimited field to the treasure hunter, since there are almost no limits to the length to which women have gone in the past—and probably will in the future—to enhance their charms, and probably the most familiar of these aids to beauty is the necklace.

Rubies, diamonds, emeralds, gold, and silver, have gone into the baubles which have encircled the necks of some of the world's most famous beauties. These necklaces of the past are well within the scope of the treasure hunter. Whether they are very ancient or comparatively modern—provided they are of fine craftsmanship or set with precious stones or can be proven to have belonged to some particularly important personage.

The necklaces of ancient Egypt were of exceptionally fine quality —and certainly are worth the treasure hunter's time. Necklaces of this period have already been found, of course; one of these finds being a serpent necklace discovered on the mummy of the royal Egyptian princess, Knoumit. The necklace was of gold, silver, and emeralds. This, naturally, was a tremendous find—but there are other Egyptian necklaces which have never been located. And, since many of the ancient tombs were desecrated and robbed and the items found therein scattered to all parts of the world, there is really no telling where you might find another treasure similar to the necklace of Princess Knoumit.

Also watch for the necklaces of ancient Crete. The British Museum already has examples of these fine necklaces, of amethyst, rock crystal, and carnelian beads, but there were others which may never be found—and others which may be found by you.

The necklaces of ancient Persia should also not be forgotten. One of the greatest finds was made near Susa in the early part of the twentieth century when Henry de Morgan discovered a sarcophagus. It contained the skeleton of a woman, and with her skeleton were many necklaces—emerald and jade and turquoise and lapis lazuli. There was also one other necklace, a three-row necklace of pearls. Originally it had consisted of over four hundred pearls, and when de Morgan found the necklace, over two hundred of the pearls were still in good condition. Who knows what other necklaces are still hidden from the eyes of mankind—waiting to be found by a treasure hunter.

With the amount of grave robbing through the ages there is no telling what you might find—anywhere—whether it is in the bazaars of the east or even here in America. Tourists have brought back stranger things than lost treasures, without even knowing what they had.

One of the objects to keep in mind—and certainly they were on the minds of beautiful women of the past—are brooches, such as the medieval brooches of the Irish and the Anglo-Saxon women. But these are not the only brooches to watch for. There are brooches from all times and all eras—from the plain and simple historic brooches to those which are of value because of their precious-stone settings.

Nor did the beauties of the past neglect their arms. They decorated them with some of the most magnificent bracelets the world has ever seen. In the time of ancient Egypt, all kinds of precious stones and enamels were used to make beautiful bracelets.

Some of these ancient Egyptian bracelets have already been found, among them the bracelets of the Queen of Zer. These are of gold and turquoise, and at least one of them is decorated with golden hawks.

There were other bracelets—those of the Persians, the Medes, the ancient Jews, and the ancient Greeks of the time of the Trojan War. All worth watching for.

Gold powder is another item to look for from this era. This, however, was used by the men of ancient Persia, who actually dusted their long, curled beards with gold powder.

Gold powder for dusting the beard may seem unusual to us, but it certainly is not as unusual, nor as beautiful, as some of the decorations of the women of long ago—all of which are listed as treasure-hunting items.

Among these must be included the forehead jewels used by the women of the Renaissance. These gems were worn in the middle of the forehead, sometimes attached to a head veil. These were beautiful then and are beautiful today—if you can find them.

These treasures of women's beauty can be found by anyone, even by a farmer who found a ring and tied it to his dog's collar. The dog wore it for over six months—until the farmer discovered that the ring was gold. It turned out that the ring had belonged to Ethelswith, sister of Alfred the Great, Queen of Mercia in the ninth century. Today this ring is a prized possession of the British Museum.

Another famous find was made in a field at Stratford-on-Avon, when the ring that Anne Hathaway allegedly gave to William Shakespeare was discovered.

The value of a ring, if you find one, is increased a great deal if it belonged to a famous person—or if the ring is set with precious stones so that it has a value of itself. But whether the ring you find is a golden ring of Mycenae, an English iconographic gold and silver ring bearing images of the Saints and made in the 15th century, an antique memorial ring, or a unique and ancient ring of any kind, it is worth while having it examined by an expert. At least don't attach it to your dog's collar.

From rings to fingernails is not a long step in beauty adornment —as the women of ancient China proved with their Manchu finger guards. These guards, protecting the long fingernails which were a sign of class status, were made of silver and gold and jade.

Whatever it is that you find, have it checked. If it was used to beautify a woman and if it is set with diamonds or emeralds or rubies, your problems are solved—no matter what famous person may have worn it. But sometimes it takes a little more to make an item of jewelry into a treasure. Such as the hairwork jewelry which was so popular during the 1800's. Made of human hair, these were bracelets, earrings, and charms for charm bracelets. Originally, hairwork jewelry was a kind of keepsake, made from the hair of a loved one who had died. But as time went on it became a fad and there was hardly anyone who did not have at least one item of hairwork jewelry. Today hairwork jewelry has a minimal value.

For example, hairwork brooches and earrings can be purchased for from $50 to $100. But, if you find examples of hairwork jewelry which had belonged to a famous person, or if the jewelry itself has an unusual history, the value of the item would naturally increase. And this is a point to remember when looking for any items used by women from time immemorial to enhance their beauty.

XXX

EAT, DRINK, AND BE MERRY

Silver, China, Spoons

CRAFTSMEN of all the ages have catered to man's necessities, and because of this the treasure hunter can search his attics, his cellars, and the second-hand stores for treasures unimaginable.

Dishes that look like junk, battered teapots, little figurines to make your tables and your rooms look prettier, silver of all kinds—all these you can find and all of them are worth money in your pocket if you will only look for them.

Silver of any kind if it was made by Paul Revere is valuable—if you can find it. Collectors and museum curators will always bid eagerly for it, paying thousands of dollars for even a goblet made by him.

One man owned a Revere goblet but thought it was only junk. However, he called in dealers to look at it. The first one offered him the current price for silver by the ounce, but the second dealer recognized it as Revere and paid him over $4,000 for it.

This does not mean that the first dealer was dishonest, but it does show that even experts can overlook lost treasures because they do not look closely enough or because they do not know which treasures are missing and therefore valuable.

These missing treasures of Paul Revere can be anywhere! A missing Revere copperplate, the one on which Massachusetts shillings were printed in 1775, was found in a junk pile in Scotland. Today it rests with the Antiquarian Society in Worcester.

How far a treasure can travel before the discerning eye of the treasure hunter spots it for what it is! Much of our early American silver, including Revere silver, was sent to England in the early days by families who remained loyal to the Crown. But much of it is still in America. Some of it is in the museums—but some of it is hiding in America's attics, waiting for the treasure hunter to find it.

On the other hand, some of the English items were sent to America. Tea caddies of this period, for example, worth from only a few dollars to several hundred dollars apiece, depending of course on age, condition, rarity, maker, etc.

The ever popular Toby jugs should be on every treasure hunter's list, for they are on every collector's list. Worth from a few dollars to $100 or more apiece, they can still be found—if you are willing to look for them.

Even the round, three-footed, cooking pots used by our ancestors in their open fireplaces can be worth something—if you will take the time to locate them.

However, in looking for American silver, caddies, and three-footed cooking pots, do not neglect items of European older make which are missing, such as the fabled Medici china!

In the late fifteen and the early sixteen hundreds Medici china —bowls, plates, vases, etc.—was made in Florence, Italy, and today there are not even fifty pieces of this magnificent china in existence—that is, unless you can find it.

Any piece of this china would truly be found treasure if you could locate it. There is no museum in the world that would not want it.

But not everyone can find Medici china. So try for Staffordshire china, made in Staffordshire and slanted toward the Pennsylvania Dutch market. Pieces of Staffordshire are rare, because in the past collectors thought very little of them and they were allowed to be lost or destroyed. Today they are not only desired but sought after by the collectors, who are more than willing to pay for whatever you can find. A piece of Staffordshire can be worth over $100—if you are lucky enough to find it. I have even seen prices quoted as high as $1,800 for one piece of rare Staffordshire.

Also watch for Lowestoft china, a rare piece of which can be worth hundreds of dollars. A rare but complete set of Lowestoft can be worth a couple of thousand—at least.

A set of Worcester china, if complete, can also be valuable. A complete set can be worth over $1,000—if complete, fine enough, and rare enough.

Also watch for Crown Derby china, any of it. If you are lucky enough you will find a rare piece, or if you are very lucky, a complete set.

Historical interest and not monetary value alone is sometimes important. There is also the excitement of finding important missing items, like the dessert service of flowers and blue and gold, with the mark "S," which belonged to George Washington. Only three pieces are known to be extant today—unless you can find the rest of them.

There is also a set of plates decorated with an eagle and initialed "G." and "M. W." for George and Martha Washington. Only one of these plates is known to be in existence. The others are lost—unless you can find them. Nor can any value be placed on Washington's missing china, until someone finds it. Perhaps it will bring a great deal and perhaps very little, depending on its condition and how badly the collectors want it.

Anything which comes out of the dining rooms or the kitchens of yesteryear can have some value, however—even if it did not belong to a president. Even such odd-sounding things as spiders and trivets have some value. Spiders and trivets are both names for a metal stand used to hold hot kettles. Used in front of fireplaces as early as the 1600's, they are today collectors' items.

Or perhaps you might find lusterware, each piece worth $50 or so—depending on condition, age, etc.—or some of the gold work of the early colonies, or Sheffield plate, which is in such demand by collectors.

Or you might find early pewter ware—items which always sell to collectors. Or, if you are very lucky, rare Chinese porcelain, sometimes worth a great deal if it is old enough, rare enough, and in fine enough condition.

Or you might find figurines, some of them worth only a few dollars, some of them worth $1,000 or more.

Any old silver, old china, or anything made for the comfort and beauty of the dining rooms and kitchens of the past has some value.

Even spoons have value, and one kind of valuable spoon is the apostle spoon! Collectors vie for these apostle spoons, which were made during the Middle Ages and which were still being made as late as the sixteenth century. Souvenirs of the birth of a child, these spoons would be presented as gifts at the christening.

Spoons were so rare at that time that when a person went visiting he was expected to bring his own—if he was wealthy enough to have one in the first place.

To give out apostle spoons made of silver was a mark of good breeding, fine birth, and social standing, in the Middle Ages, since only the wealthy could afford spoons of any kind.

The Middle Ages were filled with superstitions and not the least of these was the one that silver could drive out disease. For this reason, when a baby was born to a wealthy family, the parents had a silver spoon placed in his mouth to protect the child against illness. From this comes the expression "To be born with a silver spoon in the mouth" which even today means to be born of wealthy parents. For only the wealthy could afford a silver spoon and only the very wealthy could afford to give away apostle spoons as christening gifts.

Each of these latter spoons was dedicated to a particular apostle, and the finial [a decoration at the top of its handle] of each spoon showed a likeness of one of the apostles.

A full set of apostle spoons would consist of twelve, although occasionally there would be an extra spoon picturing Christ, and sometimes there would also be a spoon representing the Virgin.

Only one complete set of apostle spoons, all of them of the same date, is known to be in existence today. Dated 1628, this set is in the Goldsmith's Hall in London. It consists of thirteen spoons, because it includes the extra one representative of the "Master."

Even one apostle spoon is of some value—but if you should find a complete set and all of the same date, remember that only one other complete set exists today.

Whether it is china, silver or gold—if it belonged in the dining rooms and the kitchens of yesterday—it belongs in the museums of today.

XXXI

Paper Fortunes

Rare Stamps

IF there is a businessman who doubts the advisability of collecting stamps, it might be well to quote him a price brought in the recent auction of one of the great stamp collections.

The collection was so large that it was sold in sixteen different phases. The total stamps and covers had brought in $2,895,146. In any language this spells big business.

Part of this big business can be the treasure hunter's—if he knows what to look for!

Like the twenty-four-cent airmail issue of 1918. Each of the stamps of this issue is worth around $4,000—and there are thirteen of them missing. If you find one, look at the airplane in the corner. It is upside down.

Or watch for examples of the postmasters' provisionals, which were issued between March 3, 1845, the date on which Congress determined on rates of postage, and March 3, 1847, the date on which Congress determined that the Postmaster General should issue stamps.

Between these two dates the local postmasters issued their own stamps. These are the provisionals, which can make a fortune for you—if you can find them.

Watch for provisionals from such places as St. Louis, Mo.; Alexandria, Va.; New Haven, Conn.; Annapolis, Md.; Millbury, Mass.; Baltimore, Md.; Lockport, N.Y.; Boscawen, N.H.; Brattleboro, Vt., and New York, N.Y. Prices for provisional stamps and envelopes from these cities can range from a few dollars to $15,000, depending on condition, etc.

If you are lucky enough, you might find stamps worth thousands —just by remembering what to look for.

Stamp collecting is not just a hobby—it has become a national pastime. Today, in America, there are more than ten million stamp collectors. If you find a stamp, there is a buyer for it somewhere in America.

Remember, however, that with stamps, condition is the most important factor. To get a good price a stamp must be in fine condition. Also, if possible, retain the envelope. Often, the addition of the original envelope raises the value of the stamp.

Watch for any early stamp, and remember that it has not been too many years since the whole idea of postage stamps started.

Early stamps, stamps with errors in them, are all worth watching for. However, only the experts can tell whether or not a stamp is valuable. You can get some idea from stamp catalogues, but only the expert can tell whether or not the stamp you have is exactly the same and is in good enough condition to warrant the high values listed in the catalogues.

Also keep in mind the possible variation between the opinions of the experts. One stamp which I know about was valued by one expert at $1,000. Another expert valued the stamp at $750 and still another expert placed its value between $35 and $50.

If you have a stamp which you think might be valuable, take it to several experts and get all of their opinions. Needless to say, the thing to do then is to sell to the highest bidder.

Anyone can find a stamp. It takes no training or experience or courage, as some of the more adventuresome lost treasures do, such as the hidden pirate treasures or sunken ships. And you do not need to travel to find stamps. They could be anywhere—in your attic, in your basement, or stuck between the pages of a book.

Look again at any old envelope which you might find. Look through the old boxes you see at neighborhood auctions. It does not matter where you look; everyone has seen old letters and old envelopes lying around—and thrown them away thoughtlessly—and no one knows how many thousands of dollars worth of stamps have been destroyed or incinerated when disposing of "that old junk."

It might help in recognizing valuable stamps, if you can attend some of the stamp shows which are held from time to time in almost every town of any size in America. Look at the stamps on display which have value—and remember them. Buy a catalogue and check every odd or strange stamp against the displays on its pages.

Watch for errors. Sometimes, though not always, the fact that an error appears on a stamp indicates that it is valuable, and it is at least a good indication that the stamp might have value.

Above all, remember the rarest of the American stamps, among which are the twenty-four-cent airmail of 1918 with the upside down airplane and the postmasters' provisionals. Any early stamp can have value—like the 1869 fifteen-cent stamp with an upside down picture, which can be worth as high as $10,000. Or the 1869 thirty-cent stamp which has inverted flags in its design. This one can be valued as high as $8,000.

Prices, of course, depend upon age, rarity, right issue, etc., but there are so many stamps worth a great deal of money that it would be impossible to enumerate them all here.

Just remember that there is a fortune in those little pieces of paper you see on envelopes every day of the year—if you can find the right ones.

There are missing stamps which are worth $100,000 apiece—if you can find them. These are the fabled British Guianas.

Issued in 1856, these stamps are square. On the front appears a four-word inscription, easily identified if you find one.

Strangely enough, however, the best-known copy of the stamp has had its corners clipped off. And there is another strange fact about this extant British Guiana: no one knows who owns it! The possessor of the stamp wishes to remain anonymous. There was a time when rumors flew thick and fast about the stamp having been a gift to President Roosevelt, one of our most famous stamp collectors.

The President denied the rumor, and the identity of the owner still remains a mystery! Originally this unique stamp was located by a schoolboy, who sold it to an English dealer for five shillings! The stamp, however, did not rest here—or at this value. It was sold and sold again until it became a part of the world-famous Ferrary collection.

Yet once more the stamp moved on. It was willed to the Berlin Postal Museum and because of this the French government confiscated it. At that time funds were needed to finance the reparation debt of the Germans, and the French placed the British Guiana on the auction block.

Present at this now famous auction were two men, a M. Burrus, a French tobacco merchant, and Arthur Hind, an American manufacturer. Tension filled the room as other bidders fell by the wayside until only the bidding of Hinds and M. Burrus could be heard.

In total silence the bidding went higher and higher, and, when the price had reached $32,500, Hinds, the American, had won. He walked out of that auction the owner of one of the rarest stamps in the world.

He kept the British Guiana for the rest of his life, and, when he died, his wife placed it in the hands of an American stamp store. They sold it for an undisclosed price rumored to be more than $45,000.

The man who bought it now has a stamp valued at $100,000; yet, like many collectors, he remains anonymous, his name undisclosed to the public.

In his hands, anonymous though he is, is this copy of one of the rarest stamps in the world—yet there is a chance you might find another one if you look hard enough at those old envelopes in the attic trunk or in that old box of papers in the basement. You might even find it in an envelope stuck between the pages of a book as a marker. Certainly stranger things have happened in the world of philately.

The British Guiana, however, is not the only stamp to watch for. There are, for example, the Mauritius one- and two-penny stamps which are inscribed with the words "Post Office" instead of "Post Paid."

Just one of these Mauritius stamps has a value of approximately $20,000, depending on condition, etc. One collector is lucky enough to be in possession of an envelope which bears two of the Mauritius stamps. This envelope with its precious stamps is valued at $75,000.

Maybe you might be this lucky—if you look hard enough for one of these stamps which were originally issued at the direct order of a

Governor's wife. Lady Gomm needed stamps with which she might frank party invitations—and so the Mauritius one- and two-penny stamps were issued.

The stamps, however, carried an error. Where the engraver should have put "Post Paid" he put "Post Office." The error was eventually corrected, but stamps that contain the error are now listed as being among the most valuable stamps in the world —worth approximately $20,000 apiece.

There are also other stamps which can reach this value! Such as the "Missionaries," which range in value from $2,000 to $20,000, depending upon the original value of the stamp (two-cent, three-cent, etc.) and upon its condition.

These stamps were issued in the Hawaiian Islands and were called "Missionaries" obviously because the people who made the most use of them were missionaries. And they are listed as among the rarest stamps in the world—and therefore should be among the first of the stamps for the treasure hunter to watch for.

Also watch for the Swiss Cantonal stamps issued between 1843 and 1850, stamps which are ranked high in the list of most-wanted stamps.

D ID you know that there are Confederate stamps which are worth fortunes?

There are many of these rare and valuable stamps to be found on envelopes dating from the Civil War, stuck in an old desk or hidden in great-great-grandma's trunk. Certain "rebel" stamps are today considered to be among the most valuable in the philatelic world despite the fact that most Confederate stamps can today be bought for practically nothing. The Confederate government printed many stamps and today most of them are interesting to us only historically. Only a certain few have attained the status of rare stamps. They are the Confederate provisionals.

These stamps may be found hand-stamped or press-printed on many kinds of envelopes—symbol, perhaps, of a south at war. They may be found on commercial as well as homemade envelopes. Sometimes these homemade envelopes were made of maps, printed forms, or even wallpaper.

If you have a stamp on an envelope, however, that envelope should show postmarks of the town of issue. Local postmasters in the south had answered the need for Confederate stamps by issuing their own between June 1 and October 14, 1861. These stamps issued through the necessity of war are called the confederate provisionals.

Provisionals were printed wherever proper workmen and materials were available. Everyone who could print, it seems, wanted to get into the act.

On June 1, 1861, the south stopped using the stamps made by the Yankee government. It was not, however, until October 14 of that same year that their own confederate stamps appeared. It was, therefore, necessary to obtain stamps from somewhere to keep communications open. So the local towns and cities made their own. These are the Confederate Provisionals.

The states had seceded from the Union, men drew swords to fight their brothers—and Abraham Lincoln served as President!

Bitterness reigned and ripped apart a nation. There were big problems but there were also little ones! For example! How do you mail a letter without having to use a hated Yankee stamp?

J. H. Reagan, a Texan, was the confederate postmaster-general and he urgently needed workers for his new post office. By the simple expedient of writing to the Yankee post office in Washington and asking a number of clerks in the post office department there if they would not much rather work for the confederacy, he got his staff. All but two of the gentlemen accepted!

It was Mr. Reagan who set the June first date as the last day on which the southerners would use the Yankee stamp. All postmasters had to render their accounts as of that date. On the same day the postmaster-general of the Union suspended Yankee postal service in the south.

By October 14, proper Confederate stamps were available for use, yet even after this date, sometimes, these Confederate provisionals were used when the supply of regular stamps ran out.

These Confederate provisionals today bring in value "what the market will bear." But at the same time there are certain price ranges wherein a stamp may fall. A stamp is valuable depending on its rarity, its condition, and the desirability it has for the buyer. Its value can depend on many things. That is one reason why no set value can be placed on a stamp; yet it is certain that you should keep an eye out for Confederate provisional stamps and envelopes from:

Athens, Georgia; Autaugaville, Alabama.

Baton Rouge, Louisiana; Beaumont, Texas; Bridgeville, Alabama.

Danville, Virginia.

Emory, Virginia.

Franklin, North Carolina.

Goliad, Texas; Gonzales, Texas; Greenville, Alabama; Grove Hill, Alabama.

Helena, Texas.

Jetersville, Virginia.

Knoxville, Tennessee.

Lenoir, North Carolina; Livingston, Alabama.

Macon, Georgia; Marion, Virginia; Mt. Lebanon, Louisiana.

New Smyrna, Florida.

Pittsylvania C.H., Virginia; Pleasant Shade, Virginia.

Salem, Virginia; Liberty, Virginia; Salisbury, North Carolina; Spartan-burg, South Carolina.

Uniontown, Alabama.

Victoria, Texas.

Prices for some of the above stamps range from $1,000 to $15,000 apiece, depending on the original face value of the stamp, condition, etc. Of course there are more locales of this period which also issued valuable stamps but which are not listed, so if you have any southern stamp dated between June 1 and October 14, 1861, have it checked by a competent authority.

XXXII

ANYTHING THAT GLITTERS

Topaz, Amber, Pearls, Gold, Emeralds and Jade

A TEXAS rancher found a blue topaz weighing approximately seven hundred carats! This was many years ago at a spot near Mason, Texas.

Not too long ago, in Mason County, also in Texas, three men searched and worked for three days to make a topaz "find." Finally, tired and discouraged, they gave up. They put their equipment back in the car convinced that luck was against them. Yet, one woman along on the hunt decided to take a walk—and found a blue topaz weighing over two hundred carats!

A topaz can be valuable if it is a perfect stone. Finding a perfect topaz can be a lucky thing for the treasure hunter even in modern times, although in ancient times the hunter had an even more important reason to hunt topaz than we do. For the topaz not only had monetary value. It had the supposed power to avert sudden death!

In the United States we have found colorless, blue, yellow, and sherry-brown topaz. And there are more to be found—if you know where to look.

Watch for topaz at Mason County, Texas; at Topsham, Maine; at Nathrop and the Tarryall Mountains north of Lake George in Colorado; in the Thomas Mountain district of Utah, and in San Diego County, California.

Almost everywhere there is some sort of bauble to watch for—

even the organically fossilized gum on extinct trees, such as amber, a good sized lump of which can be worth as high as $1,000.

Watch for amber in Richmond County, New York; Cape Sable, Maryland; Mercer, Salem and Camden Counties, New Jersey; and in Dukes County, Massachusetts.

Also, while you are watching for topaz and amber, do not forget the pearl. You do not need to go to exotic isles or foreign shores to find pearls. You can look for them right here in your own backyard.

Precious pearls can and have been found in America. They are produced by Quadrula, a fresh-water mussel. Chances are, of course, that the fresh-water pearls you find will not have the same value as marine pearls, but fresh-water types can be precious pearls.

Watch for them in the rivers of Michigan and Wisconsin. Try the Mississippi Valley, Tennessee, Iowa and Arkansas. Watch for them in Kentucky, New Jersey and Illinois.

Way back in the 1850's a farmer was chasing a cow. His foot struck a rock which, with the impact of his foot, broke off; when he stopped to look at it he saw that it was spotted with gold. Another discovery had been made, and, before it was over, over $1,000,000 in gold had been taken out of the spot where the farmer had stumbled over the rock. And only a hundred and fifty feet away they took $4,000,000 worth of gold out of the ground!

Anyone who vacations has a chance to find gold by panning in the stream beds of the gold country. Even the boy scout on a camping trip can come home with gold. All he needs is his gold pan, a little luck—and a little knowledge.

The yellow of gold is known to everyone. To find gold in a stream is an easy thing. When you see it, you know it, instinctively. It may be shaped as a grain, a nugget or sometimes fine as sand. But it is gold.

When you are not sure of what you have, or you just want to know for sure, write to the United States Department of the Interior, Washington, D.C. They have information on gems and minerals—and if they do not have the information you want, they can tell you who to ask. However, do *not* ship them your samples of gems or gold, just *ask* for information.

There are also local gem and rock clubs for you to contact. Almost any town of any size has one of these clubs, and the members are almost always kind and courteous and willing to help.

Also write to the United States Government Printing Office, Washington 25, D.C., asking for a list of the booklets they print pertaining to gems, etc. These pamphlets are sold to the general public for a minimum fee and they contain some of the finest and most complete information.

Remember, anything that glitters is worth at least an investigation. With a rockhound's pick, a gold mining pan (even an old pie pan will work in an emergency) and the help of the United States Government, you might come home from your vacation with a fortune!

I F you can find an emerald which is of good quality and large in size (over six carats), its value would be greater than that of a diamond.

The dark green of the emerald is among the most beautiful sights on earth, especially to the finder. To find a stone of gem quality is a very rare thing, though emeralds have been found in the United States. In North Carolina there are so-called emerald mines in several areas, but they are not active. There have also been reports of emerald finds along the Bowen River in South Carolina.

It is possible that you might be the one who finds an emerald within the United States—possibly along the banks of the Bowen River. And certainly if you could spot the superb grass green of a large gem emerald, its value would be great. The grass green of the emerald is a magnificent green—but there is only one true imperial green. This is the imperial green of jade, the green which is the most highly prized although jade comes in all shades of green.

We always think of jade as being associated only with the Orient; yet not too many years ago a huge jade boulder weighing over one thousand pounds was found in California near the area of the Trinity River. The boulder was one solid mass of every shade of green imaginable—and some of it was thought to be imperial green. And in Mendocino County, California, a large deposit of jade was found.

Jade, in both varieties, jadeite and nephrite, ranges in colors from white to dark green, but the imperial green jade is the most highly desired. A necklace of matched imperial beads has been valued at $100,000.

The finding of just one piece of jade can turn family picnics into wild scrambles in search for more. Watch for both nephrite and jadeite—although jadeite is rarer and therefore has more value. But watch for both of them along the beaches and in stream beds, and also watch for deposits of jade.

Watch for the rare jadeite at the North Fork of the Eel River, Trinity County, California; Clear Creek, San Benito County and in Cloverdale and Valley Ford, Sonoma County, California.

Watch for nephrite at the North Fork of the Eel River, Trinity County, California; southeast of Lander, Wyoming; and Marin, Monterey and Tulare Counties, California.

The West seems to have all the best of it when it comes to jade hunting, but in North Carolina they have found rubies. Everyone knows the value of the ruby, especially the prized pigeon's blood color. The deep, deep red of the most highly prized rubies defies description, and the value of a fine ruby is higher than that of a diamond—if you can find it.

Watch for gem-quality rubies in stream beds and stream gravels especially. Watch for them at Cowee Valley, Macon County, North Carolina; and at Yogo Creek, Judith Basin County, Montana. Also watch for them in both Wyoming and Colorado. In Wyoming, gem rubies have been found at Marion Claim, Fremont County; in Colorado, they have been found at the Calumet mine, Salida.

If you should discover a gem similar to a ruby but which is some other color, and especially if it is a cornflower blue, do not throw it away. It may not be a ruby—but it could be a sapphire. Both rubies and sapphires are corundum—and both are worth your search. The red is ruby—but sapphire can be pink, green or yellow, salmon, cornflower blue, or colorless.

Watch for sapphires in Montana at Dry Cottonwood Creek deposit, northeast of Butte, Deer Lodge County; the Rock Creek deposit southwest of Philipsburg, Granite County; Missouri River deposits, northeast of Helena; Quartz Gulch, in Granite County; also in Chouteau County; Pole Creek, Madison County, and Browns Gulch, Silver Bow County.

Watch for sapphires in Indiana in Morgan County. In Idaho, watch for them in Washington and Adams Counties. Look for them in Colorado in Fremont County, and in California at Barstow, San Bernardino County.

Sapphires have also been found at the Calumet iron mine in

Chaffee County, Colorado, and at the Corundum Hill mine, Macon County, North Carolina, and the Sapphire and White Water mine, Jackson County, North Carolina.

You might find a cornflower blue, that most prized sapphire! Buried in the anonymous rocks of a river deposit, or coated so with dirt that unless luck is with you, you might pass it by.

This almost happened to one of the world's most famous gemstones, the Australian Andamooks Opal, now belonging to Elizabeth of England. The gem is now magnificently set as the main stone of a necklace with matching earrings. But, originally, the opal, over four inches long and two inches wide in the rough, was so dirty that not even the miners recognized it for what it was until one of them accidentally chipped it with his pick.

So if, here in America, you chance across a dirty stone but which, if you look closely, shimmers and dances with inner fires, hang on to it. It could be opal—for opal too has been found here in America.

In the state of Nevada there is a place called Virgin Valley, where at some time in the eons of the past barks of trees, pine cones, and driftwood were covered by volcanic ash. Today, if you look carefully enough, some of them have become opals.

This Virgin Valley is noted for its precious opal, the most valuable of the opal gems. Also look for precious opal in lava flows of the Columbia plateaus in Washington, Oregon and Idaho.

The so-called common opal, less rare and less valuable, can be found in Oregon, New York, Florida, New Jersey, Georgia and North Carolina.

The rarest of all the opals, of course, is the black opal, but more familiar to most of us are the white opals and the fire opals, aptly named because their inner flame resembles a rainbow fire unequalled in any other gem in the world.

The opal is known throughout the world as a "bad luck" stone, but certainly no treasure hunter would consider it bad luck to find a prize gem, an opal of fine quality. If he is extremely fortunate, however, he will find an emerald, a ruby, or a piece of imperial jade.

XXXIII

THE GOLDEN EARTH

All Kinds of Buried Treasure

BURIED treasure, usually associated with treasure hunts, is everywhere. And not just pirate treasure. In every war in America, in the Revolution, the Civil War, the numerous fights with the Indians, people hid their wealth in the walls of their homes, in their gardens, and under the front porches.

Many times they never made it back—and their family gold is still there waiting for you to find it.

In the days of the gold rushes, many of the miners hid their pokes in the walls of their shacks or back in the earth from whence it came. Between the gunfights and the brawls many of them were never able to go back for it. And it is still there—waiting for the lucky treasure hunter.

Probably the most romantic, and the hardest to discover, are the lost mines and the pirate treasures of yesterday. Anything buried beneath the earth seems to have a fascination for everyone. Who would not want to find the treasures of Blackbeard and Lafitte? Or the Lost Dutchman mine?

However, what the seeker for buried treasure usually finds is only a great deal of adventure—and very little treasure.

Many obstacles stand in the way of the buried-treasure seeker. Not the least is the fact that these treasure hunts take up a great deal of time which the average person cannot spare from his daily living. Only very rarely is there a treasure close enough to one's home, or even close enough to the surface for the average person to go hunting for it. If it is, and if you would like to make a vacation of treasure hunting, this is fine. But usually the amount of time and effort needed for a venture of this sort is out of reach of most.

But when you do go, to hunt seriously or to spend some fun time at it, check every fact for yourself. Never, never depend on facts as you read them anywhere. If you cannot travel to your treasure spot for needed research, then write to the Chamber of Commerce, the local librarian, etc.

Always, check, check and re-check any stories you hear or read about lost treasures. Legend intermingles with fact until only the authorities can unravel them.

Check your information, your legends, and your maps as carefully as you can. You cannot do too much research before you dig. Every iota of fact you gain before you start using your spade is getting you that much closer to the treasure.

Also there are laws governing the searching for—and the finding of—lost treasure. Know your laws before you dig. Always check with the territorial or state authorities in the area in which you wish to go treasure hunting. There are state laws and federal laws regarding both the finding and keeping of lost treasure.

Information of all types has to be checked. Even maps that may have been in your own family for generations may need further elucidation. Remember that the map you have may be a genuine pirate or lost mine map, but the man who had the treasure or knew where the mine was may not have plainly written down its location. He made the map in the first place because he didn't want anyone else to know where it was. Many times even authentic maps are backwards or even in code. "Step ten paces north" may mean step ten paces south. "Pass three rocks" may not mean rocks at all but trees—trees which may have come down since the day the original treasure was buried.

But if you have an authentic map and have the determination and the money, you might find treasure. Or you might find it accidentally. It has been done before.

You might find your treasure—provided, that is, that you have properly checked into the laws of the state in which you are going to search. Some states, as noted above, have their own regulations concerning the digging for treasure. In Florida, for example, the treasure hunter has to have a permit costing around a hundred dollars before he can even begin to hunt for his treasure. He gets it from the land agent in Tallahassee, and after he finds his treasure, he has to give the state of Florida 12½% of anything he finds within the territorial jurisdiction of the state.

And then, there is the income tax! Imagine the income tax on, say, Blackbeard's hoards or Jean Lafitte's treasure.

Then there are various rules, laws, and regulations concerning both buried treasure and sunken treasure. Find out about them before you start to dig or dive. Write to the Chamber of Commerce in the closest city to your treasure spot. Write to the Federal Government in Washington.

Hunting for lost mines or hidden pirate treasure is probably one of the most exciting adventures in the world. It is so far removed from the mundane existence of everyday living that even to consider it is to lift the average man's spirits. From such day dreams of lost doubloons or lost mines he goes on—to find treasure.

Probably one of the most fabulous among the buried treasures is the lost silver mine of James Bowie. Most of us remember James Bowie as the man who died beside Davy Crockett at the Alamo— but the seeker of treasure remembers him as one of America's most inveterate treasure hunters.

He was so enamored of the idea of treasure that, when he heard that the Indians knew of a vast and secret silver mine, he befriended them, he became a blood brother to them, and he lived with them. All so that he could learn the secret of their silver mine.

James Bowie found his mine, only to take the secret of its whereabouts with him when he died at the Alamo. And his silver mine is still there waiting to be found. Not too many miles from the modern city of San Antonio are the remains of an old Spanish fort near the banks of the San Saba River. It was somewhere near this fort that Bowie found his mine.

Maybe it will be there that you will find your treasure, or maybe it will be on Oak Island, where, while you dig, you will not even know what it is that you are digging for.

It happens sometimes that a treasure hunter does not know what he is looking for—only that it is treasure of some kind. Such is the treasure of Oak Island.

A small island off the coast of Nova Scotia, Oak Island is a place of mystery and hope. Every so often, ever since the year 1795, men dig there for a fortune that is buried so deeply and so well that no man has ever come close to it.

Men have tried. They have tried to the depth of one hundred and sixty feet. Every ten feet they have found a manmade obstruction. They remove it and go on. But at every attempt to reach the final treasure, water fills the diggings.

At some time in man's history someone constructed here on Oak Island a trap for the treasure hunter. The treasure is buried in such a way that water and possible death meet the digger at every turn.

It is only logical that the original treasure owners provided a "secret" method of reaching the treasure without allowing water to fill the pit, but, so far, no living man has found it. Yet we know that there is treasure there. Clues? A depression in the ground (now disappeared because of digging) where something had been buried; an ancient tree with scars of what might have been a block and tackle. Also, most important, drills have been forced into the diggings and they have churned in loose metal—and brought up some ancient golden links.

Who were the men who buried here? Not pirates, certainly, for the original diggings are far older than our history of pirates would account for. Perhaps an unknown race or perhaps some of man's early sea marauders.

Whoever they were, until today they have successfully kept hidden what is undoubtedly a vast hoard of wealth, but one can only speculate on what it is that lies there at Oak Island. There is, however, one place where so many men have buried so much treasure that it could very well be called the island of gold.

For this is legendary Cocos Island, land of rain, bad weather, and rats. The pirates who stopped here were legion. Treasure hunters today make of Cocos a place of gold and plate. It is less than five miles wide, and if all the treasure stories connected with it are true Cocos would be the richest island in the world, inch for inch.

Captain John Cook stopped at Cocos with loot. So did the pirate Benito Bonito, who hid $5,000,000 worth of treasure there. Captain Thompson, commanding the ship the "Mary Dear," which carried a cargo of wealth from Lima, Peru, buried his loot on Cocos.

There is also a possibility that Richard Davis hid treasure there. The list of pirates who supposedly hid their wealth on Cocos is endless, and no one knows how much treasure is really hidden there. All that is certain is that it is a treasure hunter's dream come true.

Another treasure hunters' paradise is in the Everglades, where Calico Jack Rackham buried millions of dollars' worth of pirate loot. The spot is ten miles up the Shark River, certainly an appropriate location for the burial of pirate gold—millions of it.

Or the treasure hunter might search for the millions buried by Edward Teach, better known as Blackbeard. Boca Raton is one place where Blackbeard is said to have buried treasure—and it has never been found, despite the countless number of searchers who have looked for it.

Then there is the treasure of the gentleman pirate Jean Lafitte. He was one pirate who had so much loot he could not bury it all in one spot. So he spread it around. Many are the tales of the loot of Jean Lafitte and many are the places where it is said he buried his treasure—as follows: (1) $20,000,000 on Caillou Island. (2) The Isle of Pines, where already two cannons have been found with jewels and gold hidden inside. (3) Honey Island. (4) The mouth of the Lavaca River, where the remains of Lafitte's ship, the "Pride," have been found in the river. (5) Kelso's Island. (6) Barataria Bay, where Lafitte had his headquarters for some time. (7) Pecan Island. (8) Grande-Terre, where Lafitte held auctions of his pirated ware. (9) Avoyelles Parish. (10) Last Island, where Lafitte fled during one of his many bouts with the United States Government. (11) Ruston, Louisiana. (12) Galveston Island (now the city of Galveston). (13) A Louisiana island in Lake Bourne. (14) Cocos Island.

Then there was the treasure of Henry Morgan! One of the most vicious of the pirates, his stopping-off places were many and varied. One of these was a place called Santa Catalina, an island near the coast of Nicaragua. There is reputed Morgan treasure at Porto Bello, a spot which Morgan captured by using his prisoners, nuns and priests, as a cover, to hide the fact that his pirates were putting scaling ladders on the walls. Once inside the city Morgan tortured and killed the inhabitants. Treasure at all costs!

There is Morgan treasure at Maracaibo, where he ravaged the city and then ran head-on into three Spanish galleons. Nothing daunted, he set fire to one galleon, made the Spaniards burn the second, and captured the third. He murdered most of the prisoners and took fifteen thousand pieces of eight from the wreck of one of the galleons.

He attacked Panama and carried away a great deal of the treasure of the old city, although it is said that he buried part of this loot on the trail out of Panama. Left, however, is treasure which Morgan was unable to find in Panama and most of which is still buried in the old city. A part of it has been found in modern times in vaults and tunnels and buried deep in the earth by the unfortunate inhabitants of Panama. Not even Morgan's great finesse in the art of human torture would force them to reveal where they had hidden it.

BUT not even the fame of the Morgan hoard can eclipse the fame of another treasure which is closer to home. This is the lost gold mine of the Superstition Mountains in Arizona.

The name of the lost mine is familiar to everyone as the "Lost Dutchman." When telling the story of this mine, Jacob Walz, sometimes called Waltzer, a German prospector and therefore nicknamed the "Dutchman," is usually mentioned.

Walz would go into the mountains and come out with gold whenever he needed it. Many people tried to follow him—and never came back. Legend says that Walz killed the men who tried to locate his mine by following him. Legend also has it that the "Dutchman" died in Phoenix in 1891—without ever leaving any information as to the location of his mine. Yet, there is another story, that he did leave information. Whatever the true facts may be, the Lost Dutchman mine has never been located.

There is, of course, the other tale—the one that states that the Dutchman had never really found a mine. The story goes that Walz let the rumors of his mine circulate merely to hide his thefts of gold from the Vulture mine, a mine which was then in operation and which was about sixty miles northwest of Phoenix. It is a known fact that gold was stolen from this mine, but whether the Dutchman stole it or whether he quite coincidentally took gold from his own private gold mine will probably never be known.

Many years before Walz, a Spanish family by the name of Peralta actually did mine gold in these mountains, and traces of the Peralta mines have been found. The story goes that the Peraltas were forced by the Apaches to abandon their mine.

The legend of the Lost Dutchman mine, too, is filled with tales of Indian vengeance, for these were the mountains where the Thunder Gods lived. To the Indians these mountains were sacred—and the pale faces had violated them.

According to the Phoenix, Arizona, Chamber of Commerce the area of the Superstition Mountains is a "wild, rough country. It is dangerous to enter the area without a competent guide."

Many people have already died because they tried to find the Lost Dutchman mine, and chances are that many more will die before either the legend is disproven or the mine is found.

Men who have looked for this gold mine have died—from getting lost, from exhaustion, from bullets fired by unseen assailants— and perhaps they died for nothing. Perhaps, after all, Jacob Walz never really found a gold mine. Or perhaps he did.

The Chamber of Commerce of Phoenix says, "Mining engineers and geologists are pretty well agreed that the Superstition Mountains are not well mineralized," yet the hunt for gold continues like a fever.

No hunter for gold ever really listens, anyway, to the authorities. He always believes that he can, and will, be the one to find the missing mine. The area where the Lost Dutchman is supposed to be is mountainous, dangerous and rough. Perhaps this is why the legends of the mine persist. The very aura of the territory gives them credence.

But for those who would really be interested and who really believe in the existence of the Lost Dutchman, there is information available. The Chamber of Commerce in Phoenix recommends the following: "For geological data and maps we suggest . . . the College of Mines, University of Arizona, Tucson, Arizona. A topographic map, the Florence, Arizona, *Quadrangle*, may be obtained from the U.S.G.S., Washington, D.C., for twenty-five cents."

There is of course really little chance—except pure luck—that anyone will ever find the lost mine. But if it ever should be discovered, it would be worth almost any effort that had been expended in finding it—short of murder.

THE Lost Dutchman would be a hard treasure to find, but at least it is here at home. But sometimes a treasure is so far away not only in terms of space but in terms of time that the tremendous effort and expense required in just looking for it are so extreme that men will probably only dream of it. It could, however, be found accidentally.

For this is the treasure of Attila the Hun! Somewhere in Europe beyond the banks of the Danube is the burial place of Attila. No one knows where, only that if it could be found it would provide untold treasure.

For when Attila, the so-called Scourge of God, was buried, into the ground with him went the spoils of his victories. His coffins alone, if they could be found, would be worth a fortune. When they buried him, they did it in their own barbaric way. He was buried in three coffins, one inside the other. One was a coffin of iron! One was a coffin of solid silver. And one was a coffin of solid gold!

Finding such an ancient treasure might not be as much of an impossibility as it would at first seem. It was in 1858 that eight gold crowns which had belonged to a Visigoth king of the 600's were found near Toledo, Spain. Historians think that the king had given these crowns to a church, but they are not definite. This is only a suggestion, but it is not important here. What is important is that they were found after having been lost for over twelve hundred years.

So it could be with the coffins of Attila the Hun, if the treasure hunter were only lucky enough to find them. Any of the giants of the lost treasures, the lost mines, the pirate treasures, the coffins of Attila the Hun may be found someday—by you!

XXXIV

Beneath the Sea

Sunken Treasure

THE amount of treasure that has been lost under the sea has been estimated at many millions of dollars. If you have dreams of sunken galleons and ships loaded with gold, then watch for old maps, old charts. And watch for money which washes up on beaches, for this is one way of telling that somewhere nearby lies a ship beneath the sea—and when storms rage and the water churns, the cargoes are moved and doubloons flee from their watery grave to be washed up on the beach.

One ship was found by using this reasoning. In the late 1700's a treasure ship sank off the coast of South Africa. Recently skin divers went down after it and found it. They found cannon and coins, evidence of a far greater treasure still to be brought up.

The ship was the Grosvenor. It carried a cargo of gold and wealth untold, including a throne that was encrusted with gems. The Grosvenor went down only one hundred yards from the shore; yet, it took men a hundred and seventy-five years to find it.

But they were certain of success, and one reason for their optimism was the fact that over the years the tides had brought in doubloons and laid them on the beach.

There is another beach where a person may find sand and pebbles—and doubloons. The sea washed up gold at Naples, Florida. Probably from an old wreck, it gives credence to the story of a Spanish galleon that went down off the coast in the latter part of the seventeenth century.

The Grosvenor has been found, but as yet not the ship off Naples. Let us hope that it does not take another one hundred and seventy-five years to find this one.

Yet the years do go by, and men have known of ships down there waiting, and the ships are still there. In 1798, a mile off Lewes, Delaware, the De Braak was sunk by a storm. Carrying eighty thousand pounds and a cargo worth over $10,000,000 she still lies at the bottom of the sea. As late as the 1930's money was found washed up on a beach near where the De Braak went down!

Whether money has been washed up from the wrecks or not, they are there waiting for you to find them if you can expend the time, the effort, and, sometimes, the courage.

The Kitty Reeves with a cargo of copper went down in Lake Huron. The Westmoreland, with at least a portion of its cargo laid out in gold, went down in the Great Lakes. And underneath the waters of Lake Erie is a ship called the Atlantic. Its cargo was gold!

Treasure ships went down everywhere, it seems. Tales of treasure in our southern waters are particularly common, especially around the coastal waters of Florida, where ships went down carrying with them untold millions of dollars in cargo.

Tales of ships down off the New England coast, however, are rare and far between, and so are the official records of these sinkings. Most of the ships bearing good cargo went down years ago, but, alas for the treasure hunter, the records are scarce. Lyle J. Holverstott, Archivist in charge, Fiscal Branch, General Records Division, the National Archives, says, "Information in records in the National Archives on shipwrecks in the New England area generally does not exist before the establishment of the Life-Saving Service in 1874."

He goes on to say, however, that there is an *Annual Report* of the Lighthouse Board and of the Life-Saving Service available to the public in most of the large libraries in America . . . and in these annual reports are frequent statistical or narrative reports on wrecks after about 1885." This is at least one source of information available on New England shipwrecks.

The main source, however, could be the lucky finding of an old letter, a newspaper, or even an old logbook—if you are lucky. Look for these old letters, old newspapers, and log books, in second-hand stores, stuck away in old desks in the second-hand stores, and even in your attic. And then use the information therein as a stepping-stone to wealth.

There are other paths to sunken treasure wealth, and, like most of them, they are to the south of us. One of these is the treasure of Silver Shoals. Off the coast of Florida, at the southern extremity of the Bahama Islands, there lie, under the water, sixteen Spanish galleons, some of them still facing toward the open seas they tried to make. Their cargo holds were filled with wealth undreamed of in jewels and gold, as they faced the double burden of terrible reefs and a violent hurricane.

Legend says that only one ship survived the storm; all the rest were rotting in their ocean grave. Such were the stories that William Phips, in another century, listened to as a young man. Listened to and believed in so strongly that he was able to convince first Charles the Second and then the Duke of Albemarle that treasure lay within their grasp.

Financed first by the king in an unsuccessful try and then by the duke on a second try, Phips located one of the treasure ships, taking back untold wealth to England. He became one of the richest men in England; he was knighted, and was made the first governor of the Massachusetts Colony.

Phips meant to go back to his treasure ship, but somehow he never did. He left over half the treasure in the ship because he feared a leakage of information—and leakage to other treasure seekers meant death to himself and to his men. So he fled to England—and a knighthood.

The rest of the treasure, however, is still there. Sixteen gold-filled Spanish galleons. They call it the Treasure of Silver Shoals, and it is marked by two reefs jutting out like the twin points of a crescent moon and another rock within the horns of the crescent.

Sometimes, however, treasure hunting is even more frustrating than this. Many years ago divers went down looking for a sunken ship in New York's East River, thirty miles north of Sandy Hook. They found an anchor, but the anchor did not belong to the ship they were looking for.

They discovered that the anchor belonged to a ship called the Hussar, a British ship which went down in the late 1700's, carrying with it four million dollars intended as pay for the redcoats.

Yet, even after they found the anchor, they did not find the Hussar. She still lies in the East River, thirty miles north of Sandy Hook —waiting for some lucky treasure hunter to bring her up.

SOMETIMES we know the exact spot of a sunken treasure but it eludes us in the deeps. In 1946, treasure seekers tried for a ship which had gone down off Key West, Florida. They were after the Spanish galleon which went down carrying Montezuma's ransom to Cortez, a treasure known to everyone. Consisting of over $20,000,000, the treasure of Montezuma to date still lies there at the bottom of the sea.

Also still at the bottom of the sea are Carlotta's rubies. The story of Maximilian and Carlotta is one of the most famous and sorrowful of any in the annals of treasure history. When Maximilian accepted the throne of Mexico in 1864, he brought his young and lovely wife Carlotta to sit beside him on the throne as Empress.

He brought her to his palace at Chapultepec, which is a hill just outside Mexico City. It means "Hill of Grasshopper" and was originally a place of worship for the ancient Aztecs. Things were not easy, however, for Maximilian, and he soon was in deep trouble.

Carlotta fled from Chapultepec, in the midst of her husband's difficulties, because she thought she would be able to get help for him in Europe, but help was refused her. She tried to get assistance from both Napoleon III and from the Pope in Rome. Both of them turned her down. When she was told that she would not be given any help for her husband, it affected her mind.

In 1868, with Carlotta still in Europe, Maximilian was at Querataro trying to defend it, but he was betrayed. He was taken prisoner, court-martialed, and executed.

When Carlotta heard the news she became completely insane, and she died eventually in seclusion in the Chateau de Bouchoute in Belgium.

The lovely young Empress, before all the trouble, had owned much beautiful jewelry, and one of the things she had brought with her to Mexico were her rubies, an especially beautiful set.

When she fled from Chapultepec, she was forced to leave the rubies behind, and, after Maximilian was tried and executed, they passed from hand to hand until finally, in 1908, the rubies were on board an east-bound ship. A storm arose, and the ship went down carrying with her Carlotta's rubies.

Today, that ship is still down, somewhere in Chesapeake Bay, waiting for the treasure hunter to come look for her and the rubies of the Empress who went mad.

There are all kinds of things under the sea, including a whole city full of treasure! In this underwater ghost town a man, with the proper equipment, could walk the lanes of yesterday and see for himself the ruins of another time when pirates walked the streets and men dealt in its shops in illicit wealth.

The City of Port Royal died on the seventh of June 1692, first groaning a little under a layer of hot air, then shivering, and finally quaking and falling into the open mouth of the sea. Today, the superstitious say that on a quiet evening if you listen closely enough you can hear the bells of Christ Church ringing down there in the sea. But the more practical man, the treasure hunter, may in a facetious vein answer the superstitious by saying that what he hears is the clinking sound of gold from a city where wealth was so fabulous that even the common man was wealthy and common taverns served their drinks in vessels of gold.

Whatever the origin of the ghostly sound, the city of Port Royal sleeps in its ocean grave, waiting for the adventurous treasure hunter to once again walk its lanes—and gather the gems and silver of another century.

But more common are the stories of ships at sea—and when speaking of the sea and its sea dogs one name cannot be overlooked: Drake! On August 20, 1558, three ships reached the Straits of Magellan, at the tip of South America. They were the "Elizabeth," the "Marigold," and the "Pelican," commanded by Sir Francis Drake.

According to *Elizabethan Sea Dogs*, by William Wood,[1] ". . . There was great store of wild-fire, chain-shot, harquebusses, pistols, corselets, bows and other like weapons in great abundance. Neither had he omitted to make provision for ornament and delight, carrying with him expert musicians, rich furniture (all the vessels for his table, yea, many belonging even to the cook-room, being of pure silver), and divers shows of all sorts of curious workmanship whereby the civility and magnificence of his native country might amongst all nations whithersoever he should come, be the more admired."

[1] From *The Chronicles of America*. Copyright Yale University Press.

Drake was so happy that all three ships had reached the Straits of Magellan safely that he changed the name of his flagship, the "Pelican," to the "Golden Hind" in honor of "the crest of his friend and patron, Sir Christopher Hatten."

The Straits of Magellan were considered to be very difficult for sailors, as navigation information concerning them was unknown. Yet, despite this difficulty of the Straits, within sixteen days Drake was almost through. Then they were actually through the Straits, only to hit a storm head on.

The storm lasted for fifty-two days, and the Marigold could not stand up against its fury, which went on and on—from September 7 to October 28, 1558. A bad omen was a two-hour eclipse of the moon, which occurred on September 15, at the very height of the storm. The Marigold went down with all hands.

The sailors said that the Marigold went down as God's punishment against a sailor named Ned Bright who was on board the ill-fated ship. Ned Bright had been the seaman who accused Daughty, another sailor, of mutiny against Drake. Daughty had been tried and executed at Drake's orders and on the evidence of Bright's testimony. The sailors believed that Ned Bright had falsely accused Daughty—therefore the judgment of God was upon him—and the Marigold went down because of it. As one sailor put it, "Marked judgment against a false witness." [2]

When the Marigold went down, she was so close to the flagship, the Golden Hind, that the men on board the latter could hear the sailors of the Marigold crying for help as they were drowning, without being able to help them.

Twenty-nine men went down with the Marigold—including Ned Bright. Yet, even after the sinking, the Golden Hind waited for the ship, in case a miracle should happen, at 30° upon the coast of Chile —a rendezvous that had been previously decided upon in case the ships were separated.

But the Marigold never came. The third ship was so damaged that they could not salvage it. They cut it up and used the pieces for firewood. This left Drake with only one ship—the "Golden Hind." But today the Marigold is still there, in the deeps, carrying a cargo of ". . . wild-fire, chain-shot, harquebusses, pistols, corselets, bows and other like weapons in great abundance. Neither had he omitted to make provision for ornament and delight, carrying with

[2] *The Life of Francis Drake*, by A. E. W. Mason.

him . . . rich furniture (all the vessels for his table, yea, many belonging even to the cook-room, being of pure silver), and divers shows of all sorts of curious workmanship whereby the civility and magnificence of his native country might amongst all nations whithersoever he should come, be the more admired." We would be happy to have the chance to admire today—if we could only bring them up again.

Some men spend their lives working with sunken treasures, and one of these is Arthur McKee. Mr. McKee is a deep-sea diver, treasure hunter, and museum curator. His Museum of Sunken Treasure is at Treasure Harbor, Plantation Key, Florida, five miles south of Tavernier, Florida, on U.S. Route 1.

A treasure hunter must have some idea of what he is looking for, and one of the best places in the United States to see articles connected with treasure hunting is McKee's museum in Florida.

One thing which tourists insist upon seeing is the view through a glass-bottomed boat, through which they can watch deep-sea divers at work on the wreck site of an ancient Spanish galleon.

McKee's museum features treasure taken from the depths of the ocean, including doubloons, cannons and cannon balls, idols, and even ivory elephant tusks from the wreck of an African slaver.

Among other things, McKee has discovered the wreck of an ancient Spanish galleon which sank off Plantation Key in 1733. A painting of this discovery today hangs in the museum.

One object brought up by McKee from the ocean depths was a seventy-five-pound bar of coral-encrusted bullion—one of three which he recovered from the rotted hull of an ancient Spanish galleon wrecked on a reef east of Key Largo. The Smithsonian Institute in Washington, D.C., bought one of these bars, paying $1,000 for it. The other two bars can still be seen in McKee's Museum.

Every man can look at found treasure while he dreams of the loot of pirates hidden on some far-off island. Or he dreams of the lost mine of Bowie or of the "Dutchman" Jacob Walz. Sometimes he possesses a map which he hopes is authentic, or he has information gleaned from some old-timer who is old enough to remember the tales of treasure he heard first-hand when he was in his youth.

When you decide to go after this kind of buried or sunken treasure, there are several places where you can get more information.

The Library of Congress can usually furnish you with some; your local library has books, usually lots of them, on sunken and buried treasure; the Chambers of Commerce of the various towns near the coasts will give you information. And you can do your own research, if you have the time to travel to your favorite treasure spot.

It's most important to know your facts before you actually start digging or diving for your treasure. Know as closely as possible where it is. Know as much historical background about it as you can. But, above all, know what it is that you are looking for. It would be ironic if you did not recognize treasure when you found it!

Suppose you were like the fisherman who, while fishing off the coast of Florida on a warm, sunny day, fell asleep in his boat. He awoke suddenly, not due to the motion, but rather due to the stillness of the boat. Rubbing his eyes, he discovered that his boat had become stuck on a reef.

The reef was spotted with coral-covered bars and he took two of them to use as ballast and shoved off. Never thinking that he would want to find that particular reef again he did not take any special notice of its location. He would have given anything to find it again two years later when he discovered that the two bars he was still using as ballast were actually solid silver—part of a cargo of $5,000,000 in silver bars which had gone down off the coast.

The story goes that the fisherman is still looking for his silver-studded reef, but he has not found it again. Perhaps someone else should try fishing in those waters on a lazy summer day—provided, of course, he knows a lost treasure when he finds one.

BIBLIOGRAPHY

American Catalog and Standard Premium List of All United States Coins

American Figureheads and Their Carvers, by Pauline A. Pinckney, Norton

American Fire Marks, Insurance Co. of North America Collection

The Andamooka Opal, by John D. Altmann, *Gems & Minerals Magazine*

Anything for a Laugh, by Bennett Cerf, Bantam Books

Antique Collecting For Everyone, by Katherine Morrison McClinton, McGraw-Hill Co.

Antiques, by Peter Hildreth, Arco Publishing Company, Inc.

Antique Guns, by Hank W. Bowman, Arco Publishing Company, Inc.

Antique Pistol Collecting—1400-1860, by James Firth and Ronald Andrews, Arco Publishing Company, Inc.

Arco Gun Book, Larry Koller, Editor, Arco Publishing Company, Inc.

The Aristocratic Ruby, by Alma J. Minai, *Gems & Minerals Magazine*

Arizona Place Names, by Will C. Barnes

Arkansas Diamond, by Earl Tobin, *Gems & Minerals Magazine*

Art of Carl Fabergé, by A. Kenneth Snowman, Faber and Faber Ltd.

The Authenticity of The Chalice of Antioch, by James J. Rorimer, Princeton Press

Autobiography of Benvenuto Cellini, Translated by John Addington Symond, Scribner's

A Bibliography of First Printings of the Writings of Edgar Allan Poe, Hattiesburg, Miss., The Book Farm

A Biographical Dictionary of The Fine Arts, by S. Sponer, Holt

Book About a Thousand Things, by George Stimpson, Harper Brothers

Bookmen's Bedlam of Literary Oddities, an olio, by Walter Hart Blumenthal, Rutgers University Press

Book of American Indians, by Ralph B. Raphael, Arco Publishing Company, Inc.

Book of Knowledge, the Grolier Society

Books on Watchmaking and Timepieces, by the Department of Commerce, National Bureau of Standards

Brief Chronological History of the Seth Thomas Company

British Military Firearms, by Howard L. Blackmore, Arco Publishing Company, Inc.

British Table and Ornamental Glass, by L. M. Angus-Butterworth, Arco Publishing Company, Inc.

Buried Treasure, by Ken Krippene, Permabooks

California State Numismatic Association Convention Auction Sale Catalog, 1957

California Yesterdays, by Irmagarde Richards, California State Dept. of Education

Chamber of Commerce Brochure, Phoenix, Arizona

A Child's Book of Gems & Minerals, by Valene Swenson, Maxton Publisher Inc.

Child's History of California, by Enola Flower, California State Dept. of Education

China Collecting in America, by Alice Morse Earle, Empire State Book Co.

Collecting Minerals, The Americana Institute

Collectors' Guns, by Don Myrns, Arco Publishing Company, Inc.

Colt Gun Book, by Lucian Cary, Arco Publishing Company, Inc.

The Complete Button Book, Lillian Smith Albert and Kathryn Kent, Doubleday

Counterfeit, Mis-Struck and Unofficial U.S. Coins, by Don Taxay, Arco Publishing Company, Inc.

Diamond, The King of Gems, by William J. Thomas, *Gems & Minerals Magazine*

Doubloons, by Charles B. Driscoll, Pennant Books

Drake, Sir Francis, Dictionary of National Biography, by John Knox Laughton, Oxford University Press

Early American Antique Furniture, by Morton Yarmon, Fawcett

Elizabethan Sea Dogs, by William Wood, Yale University

Encyclopedia Americana, Americana Corp.

Encyclopedia Americana Annual, for 1959, American Corp.

Encyclopedia Britannica, Encyclopedia Britannica Inc.

England, by John Richard Green, The Co-operative Publication Society

English Pistols and Revolvers, by J. N. George, Arco Publishing Company, Inc.

Exploring The World of Gems, by W. F. Toskog, *National Geographic Magazine*

Family Cyclopedia of Useful Knowledge

Famous Guns from Famous Collections, by Hank W. Bowman, Arco Publishing Company, Inc.

Famous Guns from the Winchester Collection, by Hank W. Bowman, Arco Publishing Company, Inc.

Famous Old Cars, by Hank W. Bowman, Arco Publishing Company, Inc.

Footprints of Assurance, by Alwin E. Bulau, Macmillan

From Broad Glass to Cut Crystal, by D. R. Guttery, Arco Publishing Company, Inc.

Gems and Gem Materials, by Edward Henry Kraus and Chester Baker Slawson, McGraw-Hill

Gems & Minerals Magazine, Mineral Notes and News

Gem Stones of the United States, by Dorothy M. Sclegel, Geological Survey Bulletin 1042-G, United States Printing Office

The Gem Trader, by Louis Kornitzer, Sheridan House

Germany, by Wolfgang Menzel, Co-operative Publication Society

Gilbert and Sullivan Book, by Leslie Baily, Cassell

Grove's Dictionary of Music and Musicians

The Gutenberg Bible, Brochure on the Library of Congress' copy of the Gutenberg Bible.

Handbooks of Popular Antiques, by Katherine Morrison McClinton, Random House

History of Postage Stamps, Postal Cards and Stamped Envelopes, United States Post Office Department

The History of the Decline and Fall of the Roman Empire, by Edward Gibbon, Wise and Co.

A History of The United States, by Ephraim Douglass Adams and John C. Almack, Harper

How and Where to Find the Facts, by William Sunners, Arco Publishing Company, Inc.

Incunabula and Americana, 1450-1800, A Key to Bibliographical Study, by Margaret Bingham Stillwell, Columbia University Press

Index of American Design, by Erwin O. Christensen, Macmillan

Information Roundup, by George. Stimpson, Harper

International Encyclopedia of Illustrations, Arco Publishing Company, Inc.

The Jeweled Trail, by Louis Kornitzer, Sheridan House

Jerusalem, by Prof. Michael Avi-Youah, Arco Publishing Company, Inc.

The Junk Snupper, by C. R. Clifford, Macmillan

A Key To Precious Stones, by L. J. Spencer, Blackie and Son Ltd.

The Life of Benvenuto Cellini, Translated by John Addington Symond, Scribner's

Life of Cesare Borgia, by Rafael Sabatini, Riverside Press

Life of Sir Francis Drake, by Alfred Edward Woodley Mason, Doubleday

Lincoln Lore, Bulletins of the Lincoln Historical Research Foundation

Madame Tussaud's Guide to Biographies (brochure)

Mann's Pictorial Dictionary and Cyclopedia, Arco Publishing Company, Inc.

The Many Sided Diamond, by George S. Surtzer, *National Geographic*

Les Medailleurs de la Renaissance, by Alois Heiss, Paris, J. Rothschild

Michelangelo, by Garden City Books

National Geographic Magazine

The Naval Side of British History, Geoffrey Callender

Old Silver and Old Sheffield Plate, by Howard Pitcher Okiem, Doubleday

Old Time Steam Cars, by John Bentley, Arco Publishing Company, Inc.

Opal Mining at Andamooka, by John D. Altmann, *Gems & Minerals Magazine*

Opals Are Easy To Cut & Polish, by J. Lester, *Gems & Minerals Magazine*

Practical Books of American Silver, by Edward Wenham, Lippincott

Practical Books of Chinaware, by Harold Donaldson, Eberlein, and Roger Wearne Ramsdell, Halcyon House

The Renaissance of Art In Italy, by Leader Scott, Scribner's

Report from the Boston Commandant to the Bureau of Construction and Repair, November 27, 1931, research memorandum

Report of the American Commission for the Protection and Salvage of Artistic and Historic Monuments in War Areas, 1946, United States Government Historical Reports on War Administration

Retail Values of Mechanical and Semi-Mechanical Banks, by Thomas H. Kenny, Jr.

The Romance of Time, by Brooks Palmer, Clock Manufacturers Assoc. of America, Inc.

Selected Bibliogaphy On Diamonds, United States Department of the Interior

Seth Thomas Clocks, General Time Corp.

Some Notes on Opal, by Ralph W. Dretz, *Gems & Minerals Magazine*

Some Outstanding Clocks Over Seven Hundred Years–1250-1950, by H. Alan Lloyd, Arco Publishing Company, Inc.

Stiegel Glass, by Frederick William Hunter, A.M., Dover Publications

Travellers' Tales, Everybody's Vacation Publishing Co.

The Twenty Six Letters, by Oscar Ogg, Crowell

United States Stamp Catalogue, Scott Publications

Victorian Jewellery, by Margaret Flower, Duell, Sloan and Pearce

Wilson's American Book and Standard Premium List of All United States Coins

World Book Encyclopedia, Field Enterprise Educational Corp.

World Book Encyclopedia Reference Library, Chicago, Illinois

World Scope Encyclopedia, Holst

INDEX